SEA AND EARTH

The Life of Rachel Carson

SEA AND EARTH

· *The Life of Rachel Carson* ·

by PHILIP STERLING

ILLUSTRATED WITH PHOTOGRAPHS

THOMAS Y. CROWELL COMPANY · NEW YORK

For Ed
Who Wanted the World
To Be Fit to Live In

· *Women of America* ·

MILTON MELTZER, *Editor*

SEA AND EARTH
The Life of Rachel Carson
   By Philip Sterling

TONGUE OF FLAME
The Life of Lydia Maria Child
   By Milton Meltzer

LABOR'S DEFIANT LADY
The Story of Mother Jones
   By Irving Werstein

QUEEN OF POPULISTS
The Story of Mary Elizabeth Lease
   By Richard Stiller

PROBING THE UNKNOWN
The Story of Dr. Florence Sabin
   By Mary Kay Phelan

MARGARET SANGER
Pioneer of Birth Control
   By Lawrence Lader and Milton Meltzer

SOMEBODY'S ANGEL CHILD
The Story of Bessie Smith
   By Carman Moore

THE SENATOR FROM MAINE
Margaret Chase Smith
   By Alice Fleming

NEIGHBOR TO THE WORLD
The Story of Lillian Wald
   By Irvin Block

ACKNOWLEDGMENTS

I am especially and irredeemably indebted to seven individuals whose relationships with Rachel Carson were among the longest-lasting and the most meaningful of her lifetime.

Robert McLean Carson was painstaking and diligent in his word pictures of the Carson family's life in Springdale and Stemmer's Run. Nor did he stint time and effort in digging out photographs and memorabilia.

Bob Hines spoke to me with an artist's gift for recognizing significant detail about his years as Miss Carson's colleague in the Fish and Wildlife Service and their work together on *The Edge of the Sea*.

Dorothy Freeman (who became Mrs. Arthur Rand in 1968) did far more than tell me the story of Miss Carson's years in Maine. She admitted me to the closeness and warmth of their friendship and thereby greatly enriched my understanding of her friend's personality. I am grateful also for the valuable photographs she provided.

Elmer Higgins helped me see Miss Carson through the eyes of a scientist-administrator, whose duty it was to judge her performance as a worker and her competence as a biologist.

Mary Frye (Mrs. J. Allan) Llewellyn and Dorothy Thompson (Mrs. Charles) Seif were especially informative about the details of their schoolmate's transition from literature to science at Chatham College and her graduate studies at Woods Hole and Johns Hopkins University.

Ruth (Mrs. Robert I.) Swisshelm, a classmate of Miss Carson and for many years director of alumnae affairs at Chatham, was resourceful and gracious beyond the call of duty in answering questions and providing documentary materials.

I also wish to thank Josephine R. Shotwell for making available her own bibliography of writings by and about Rachel Carson.

For a wide variety of help and for the generosity with which it was given, I am happily obliged to many other individuals and institutions in various parts of the country. My debt to them is recorded in the Selected List of Sources or is directly indicated in the text.

CONTENTS

THE LADY AND THE SENATORS

*A great debate has been raging . . .
over the issue posed by pesticides
. . . . Last night the nation saw an
outstanding television program, "The
Silent Spring of Rachel Carson." It
dramatically pointed up one of the
great challenges of our time—man's
assault on his environment . . . .*

—HUBERT H. HUMPHREY, MINNESOTA,
IN THE UNITED STATES SENATE,
APRIL 4, 1963

"Miss Carson," said the senator, "on behalf of the
committee, we certainly welcome you here. You are
the lady who started all of this . . . . "

Sitting at the long witness table, she looked small,
middle-aged, harmless. Her appearance gave no hint
that she might indeed be capable of starting anything
big enough to interest the Senate of the United States.
Nevertheless, no American newspaper reader could
be ignorant of what she *had* started a year earlier.

The large hearing room was crowded that June 4
morning of 1963. The 125 spectator seats were filled

with people eager to hear her testimony before the Senate subcommittee studying "Activities Relating to the Use of Pesticides." Reporters worked elbow to elbow at the press table. Photographers and television men crouched in the aisle. Three other senators were in their places at the committee table.

The speaker, Senator Abraham Ribicoff, continued: "There is no doubt in the mind of any American today that we are dealing with a very serious and complicated problem . . . . "

No one knew that better than Rachel Carson. It was her book, *Silent Spring,* that had jolted the whole country into worried awareness of the problem. She had written: "Along with the possibility of the extinction of mankind by nuclear war, the central problem of our age has become the contamination of man's total environment with substances of incredible potential for harm . . . . "

The rest of the book was a catalog of the causes for alarm, and a solemn warning: unless *Homo sapiens,* the learned ape, began to use his knowledge wisely instead of recklessly, his final scientific achievement might well be the total destruction of his kind.

" . . . There is a great void in the information," said the senator. "We are dealing here with many forces which people say are still mysterious . . . . "

Rachel Carson was a woman soundly learned in the life sciences. She was a writer gifted with more than a touch of the poet and famous for three books which revealed and explained the oceans' mysteries. Her work had been highly praised by scientists and literary critics alike. It had been rewarded by honorary degrees from half a dozen universities.

Silent Spring, in which she chose to examine mysteries of another kind, made her the target of all-out attack by powerful business interests. Officials and scientists in government agencies she had criticized tried to discredit the book. For a year, despite failing health, she had defended herself so ably and vigorously that the weight of public opinion was on her side.

The senator talked on: " . . . I think that all the people in this country and around the world owe you a debt of gratitude for your writings and your actions toward making the atmosphere and the environment safe for habitation . . . . We welcome you here. Will you please proceed as you see fit."

She did. It was her life-style to proceed as she saw fit, if she could do so in good conscience. Always. From the very beginning . . .

LAND BY THE RIVER

*Every bird speaks to me, every tree
nods gently to me.*

—John James Audubon

In Springdale, Pennsylvania, where Rachel Carson was born on May 27, 1907, people were not in the habit of asking deep questions about anything. The town sat, quietly satisfied with itself, on a small strip of land hugged by a U-shaped curve of the great watercourse the Indians called Allegheny. In their language it meant Beautiful River.

The river's 325 miles of bends and curlicues began in north central Pennsylvania, ran northwest across the New York boundary, then turned southwest to Pittsburgh. There it joined with the Monongahela to form the beginning of a greater, more beautiful river, the Ohio, which flowed for almost a thousand miles, westward with a strong southerly slant, to join the Mississippi, Father of Waters.

By 1900 little remained of the lower Allegheny Valley's original beauty except the sound of the Indian name. Gone were the first great forests of honey

4

locust, hickory, sycamore, chestnut. No such tree remained as the giant described 150 years earlier by
Father Bonnecamp, a pioneer Pennsylvania traveler.
("We dined in a hollow cottonwood tree in which 29
men could be ranged side by side.") The bear, otter,
beaver, marten, wildcat, the elk that sometimes
mingled tamely with the settlers' cows, were gone
from the land. So were the "clouds of owls" and the
flocks of turkeys almost too fat to fly. No one in the
Carsons' time could take "thirty barrels of fish in a
single cast of the net," as an Allegheny fisherman had
done in 1823.

River, land, and wildlife were shadows of their
former selves. Still, generous patches of relatively un-
spoiled earth remained. In 1900 Robert Warden
Carson found sixty-five heavily wooded acres there
at very little per acre. This big chunk of Springdale, eighteen miles upstream from Pittsburgh, still
looked, sounded, and smelled as real Pennsylvania
countryside should.

Beyond the Carson property lay the larger, less
pleasant expanse of southwestern Pennsylvania. It
was a realm of coal mining, iron smelting, and steel
fabrication; of glass, paint, aluminum, and chemical
manufacturing; of river and railroad traffic moving
endlessly in with raw materials, endlessly out with
finished goods. For those who earned their living in
factories, mines, or mills, it was a province of shabby
houses, skimpy wages, industrial accidents, unemployment, debt, and "labor troubles."

American industry did not go about its business

barefoot. For more than a century, its work boots had left deep, ugly prints on the face of the region. Maria Carson, Rachel's mother, could see them leaving new and larger ones from year to year. She was not against industry. She just felt that man, making nature ugly for the best reasons or the worst, was making his own life ugly, though he got enough to eat, wore stout clothing, and slept under a weathertight roof. Mrs. Carson's feeling was no more clearly defined than that, but it was powerful. She wanted to shield her little daughter against the ugliness of a despoiled environment. She could do it only by sharing her own loving knowledge of nature with the child. This sharing began with the song of a meadowlark.

Feeding her two-year-old daughter on the back porch one day, Maria Carson said, "Listen, Rachel. Do you hear that?" The child tilted her head obediently, tried to listen, then reached for the spoon in her mother's hand. Mrs. Carson, smiling fondly, understood that no birdsong could keep her small daughter's mind off the sweet smell of porridge for more than a few moments. But the moments grew longer as the girl grew older. She learned, and the pleasure of learning remained a strong, bright bond in the lifelong friendship of child and mother.

The back porch became Rachel's starting place for exploring the woods and fields of the Carson homestead. She discovered soon, as all young children do, that she shared the earth with creatures bewilderingly different than she was, yet amazingly like her in some ways. They were all alive. They all needed air, water, food, and some kind of shelter.

Lying in a sun-baked meadow, she watched the disorderly traffic of ants trudging to and from their "house," getting in each other's way, on errands that were a total mystery to her. Climbing a tree she looked at baby robins huddled helplessly in their nest, eyes shut tight, beaks wide open. On the ground again, she was careful not to trample the bits of pale blue eggshell the mother bird had thrown out.

A hollow drrrrr-rat-tat-tat of a sound made her look up toward a distant treetop in which some woodpecker was digging his dinner. The chirping of crickets, the shrilling of grasshoppers hidden in the grass, made her look down. The soundless flight of orange-and-black monarch butterflies made her stare straight ahead. They flew slowly, heavily, as though summer would never end. And Rachel stared and stared, dreamy-eyed, through the bright air at daisies and buttercups and at nothing at all until the light broke into tiny dots which danced before her eyes like fine raindrops on clean window glass.

Closer to home, Rachel had daily chances to meet some of the creatures man cultivates for his own special reasons. Her father felt that whether he farmed his acres or not, he ought to have some livestock on them: a cow to supply milk, pigs to butcher and store in the smokehouse, chickens for eggs and Sunday dinners, rabbits for no particular purpose. There was always a horse, of course, to pull a wagon on weekdays and a light carriage on Sunday.

None of these were as mysterious or exciting as the raccoons that quarreled loudly beyond Rachel's window in the autumn nights, or the possum that sometimes waddled out of her way on the road at dusk. But they were more fun, these farm animals. They could be looked at, cared for, even talked to, if one did not expect an answer. When Maria Carson carried a pail of cracked corn outdoors to feed the chickens, Rachel, just four, volunteered to help, flinging handfuls of food toward the birds. The bobbing motion of their heads as their beaks snapped the kernels from the ground delighted her.

Pigs were interesting, too. She couldn't tell why exactly, but there was something about them. They weren't as handsome as the horses, but they weren't as frighteningly large, either. They were dozens of times smarter than those brainless chickens that never seemed to know where they were going or what they were squawking about. And in spite of their funny looks, pigs had more "personality" than rabbits. Sometimes they seemed almost to be smiling.

Most of them got along very well with Rachel's little dog, Candy. Often the dog would climb aboard a pig that was crouching flat on the ground, at rest, and make itself comfortable just back of the animal's soft, broad shoulders. Usually the pig didn't mind. It went on resting and grunting until it felt like standing up. When it did, Candy just naturally slid off. If Rachel was nearby, she would call the dog. Then the two of them would wander among the lights, shadows, sounds, and smells of midsummer.

These were summers that seemed to last forever, the moment of their beginning too far gone to remember, their ending too gradual to notice. They were times when the passage of time could not be believed, when only the great adventure of getting acquainted with the living world was real.

THIS DOOR FIRST

. . . Millions of women in this country are condemned to the most menial drudgery . . . . But let one aspire to use her mental powers—and O! What a fainting fit Mr. Propriety has taken! Just to think that "one of the deah creatures" should forsake the woman's sphere.

—JANE SWISSHELM

Some children go to their first day at school drifting and dreaming, others go kicking and screaming. Not Rachel. At six she went quietly, eagerly, with eyes and ears wide open to soak up what was new in her life. Weeks of family talk ahead of time had churned her curiosity.

Going off to school was something to think about. It was a step toward being accepted as an equal by big-sister Marian, ten years older, and by big-brother Robert, eight years older. It was a family event and she was the most important person in it. Just the same she felt a certain uneasiness. She had never had many playmates her own age because the Carsons lived pretty much off by themselves. Their house stood

alone on Colfax Lane more than halfway up the hill
from Pittsburgh Street, at the edge of town. Though
her mother assured her it would be great fun to meet
new children, Rachel had her doubts about meeting
so many, all at once. She liked people singly, but she
wasn't sure she would like them in bunches. Brother
could be fun sometimes . . .

"What's that, Robert? Are you making something?"

"Yes."

"What?"

"A crystal-detector radio receiver."

"Oh . . . "

That took care of the conversation. But it was
interesting to hang around and watch him tinker
with wires, pliers, and cardboard cylinders. And it
was fun to find Marian in the parlor and watch her
practice a two-step to the tune of a new popular song
—*dum,* te-dum, tee-*dee*-dee ("Oh, it's you Rachel,
hi") *dum,* te-dum, tee-*dee*-dee, *wait*-in' for the *Ro*-
bert E. *Lee*-eeeeeee.

Sometimes Rachel walked with her father among
the apple trees of their ten-acre orchard that began a
short distance beyond their back door. And once or
twice she had gone with him on much longer walks
across the Carson property. Atop hilly places he stood
still, looked around, and made notes on a scratch pad.
That part of it wasn't exactly fun, but it made her feel
rather grown up to walk with him.

Yet even her own family wasn't fun to be with all
the time. She liked to be alone when she was busy

thinking about all the things she knew—ants, plants, bees, trees, possums, blossoms, raccoons, moons. Would she have any time for this kind of silent, all-by-herself thinking in school? She couldn't tell but . . .

"You're going to learn to read and spell and write, Rachel. You'll like that, won't you?"

Yes. Definitely. She would. She was getting a little tired of being teased by the word-filled, printed pages of the books in the Carsons' parlor library. Her mother encouraged her to handle them, look at them, spell out words. They were good companions, especially on bad-weather days. She liked turning the pages carefully, slowly, until she had looked at all the pictures twice, then . . . Huh! What was the use of being able to spell out some of the words if you couldn't read the rest of the words around them? So Rachel and her mother walked side by side one September morning in 1913—the little girl looking forward to her first day at Springdale Grammar School, the woman looking back at her lifetime, and remembering . . .

The world to which Maria Carson was born in Cleveland, Ohio, in 1869 was a man's world. Considering all women to be mentally and physically inferior, it did not make room readily or willingly for even the most unusual of women. No matter how exceptional their talents or abilities, they were expected to lead a life that went like this:

A woman was born, brought up, and given as much

education as her parents could afford or as little as they thought was necessary. She married, had babies, and brought *them* up. She did all the household work —cooking, baking, sweeping, dusting, laundering, sewing, nursing, canning fruits and vegetables for the winter months. On Sundays she took enough time off to sing in the choir, if she could sing. Her husband made all of the big decisions about their life, and many of the small ones.

The married "average woman" didn't amount to much legally, either. She had few independent property rights. If she was a wage earner her pay envelope as well as her heart belonged to her husband. She couldn't vote, except in Wyoming. Most married women worked like truck horses, and many of them had more sense than their menfolk. Yet they were willing to accept the idea that they ought not and could not do any kind of "man's work" in the world outside. If they did, they would be "competing" with men, which would make them unwomanly, unlady-like, unfeminine, and un–so forth and so on.

Take Maria Carson's own case. There is no way of knowing exactly what she thought about women's supposed inferiority to men. If she did disagree with the idea, she probably kept her opinion to herself, as most women did. But she had no reason to *feel* inferior.

Her father, the Reverend Daniel McBane Mc-Lean, died of tuberculosis at the age of forty, while he was pastor of the Chartiers United Presbyterian Church in Cannonsburg, Pennsylvania. Maria was only eleven then, and her sister Ida was fourteen. They and their mother, Rachel Frazier Andrews McLean, learned to manage their own affairs. They moved to the nearby town of Washington, Pennsylvania, where both girls attended the Washington Female Seminary, a United Presbyterian school. After her graduation, Ida became a piano teacher. Maria was graduated two years later, in 1887, with special honors in Latin.

Talented as a pianist and singer, she became a member of the Washington Quintette Club. In a printed program of one of the group's recitals she was listed as Miss M. F. McLean, alto. A high point of the evening had been her vocal solo, "In Old Madrid." That was in June 1891, when she was twenty-three, teaching school, and still unmarried.

No minister's daughter would think of becoming a professional performing artist in those days. And composing songs and other music, of which Maria did dream once in a while, was a very uncertain way of earning a living. Schoolteaching, on the other hand, was respectable and safe. And Maria enjoyed it. But there came a time when a girl had to choose between the three R's and the big M for marriage. She couldn't have both. Most schools had a rule against hiring married teachers. Anyway, no man who wanted to hold up his head in the world could allow his wife to work.

It was an easy choice for young Maria McLean to make when Robert Warden Carson came to town from Pittsburgh with a traveling church quartet. He was a quiet man, sturdily built. His dark, rugged good looks were accented by a massive, well-groomed mustache that few other men could have worn with such good effect. The maidenly independence Miss McLean had enjoyed since her graduation from the seminary quickly lost its importance to her. She became Maria Carson in June 1894.

Well, no regrets. If she had ever felt cramped by her "average woman's" role as housewife in a man's world, she felt no such thing while walking her small daughter to school that September morning. True, it was still a man's world. It would continue to be, but she had seen it change a good deal since she was a girl. It was bound to go on changing.

The world was making a little more room, a little less grudgingly for women—not only as students and teachers but as professionals in medicine, law, social service, journalism, and in state and federal government work. Mrs. Carson was sure that new doors would open and old ones swing wider for the women of Rachel's generation. Which would be Rachel's door? She was too wise to guess or to wish. The doors of the world were many. Better take one at a time, beginning with the door to the first-grade classroom.

A LETTER FROM ST. NICHOLAS

It wasn't that Mrs. Carson hoped; *she* saw *what Rachel had.*

—Mrs. Minerva Baker

Rachel's early years of schooling were interrupted by long, repeated absences. Miss Ocie Greasley, her second-grade teacher, could mark her present only sixteen days in the first three months of the fall 1914 term. Miss Cora P. Walters, who taught Rachel in the third and fourth grades, shook her head with concern for the girl's poor attendance record. So did Miss Elizabeth Mellon in the fifth and sixth grades.

They were always pleasantly surprised, however, when Rachel returned. She not only managed to keep up with her work but made a better showing than most of her schoolmates who had never missed a day. After a month-long absence in the fourth grade, her marks dropped considerably, but she ended the year with a B average.

"We used to say her mother did all her homework for her," one girl recalled in later years. "We knew it wasn't true, of course. When Rachel was called on to recite in class, she was always prepared. She didn't

16

flounder. What Mrs. Carson did was harder and perfectly fair. She tutored Rachel, so that her absences didn't make much difference."

It wasn't always her own illness that put blots on the little Carson girl's attendance record. When there was "a lot of sickness going around," Mrs. Carson played it safe. She kept Rachel at home for protection against the "catching" disease of the month. Maybe she played it too safe sometimes. Nevertheless, childhood diseases were a source of serious seasonal worry to many mothers besides Rachel's.

Diptheria, which Robert survived, and scarlet fever, which Rachel had, were feared as child-killers. So were typhoid fever, whooping cough, and measles. Less frightening ailments such as chicken pox, mumps, tonsilitis, chest infections, and severe colds sometimes led to fatal "complications." There were no antibiotics or sulfa drugs and no dependable preventive "shots," except anti-smallpox vaccination.

Mrs. Carson was also inclined to play it safe against heavy, deep-drifting snowfalls in Springdale's streets. On such days, when sharp frost clawed at everything outdoors, she was apt to keep her daughter at home. In less menacing weather, Rachel and Robert often shortened their three-fifths-of-a-mile walk to School Street by going the back way, across the Moyer property, which bordered theirs.

Rachel didn't mind staying home when she had to, though she liked going to school when she could. In both places she soaked up the English language as steadily and quietly as a clam straining seawater. Be-

fore she left the first grade she could feel the satisfaction of following lines of words across the pages of her
primer . . .

> Does a dog eat fruit?
> No. A dog does not eat fruit.
> Does it make him ill?
> No. It does not make him ill.
> Dogs do not like to eat fruit . . .

She learned to write and to spell—how to shape
letters of the alphabet with a pencil in her hand, how
to string letters together to form words, and how to
use the words to say things on paper. What things?
That dogs do not eat fruit? No. Who cared about
that? Rachel found herself wanting to say anything
and everything that made sense to her in ways that
would interest others. She wanted to express
thoughts and feelings, to tell stories, write poems.

On one of her out-of-school days, Rachel made a
"book" of pictures and rhymes for her father, with his
name, "R. W. Carson," in clumsy second-grade block
letters on the cover. On the other pages there were
drawings of small birds or animals. Each was accompanied by a two-line jingle using the kind of rhymes
that come naturally to children who enjoy words for
their own sake: mouse and house, frog and log, pup
and cup. There was even a drawing of a rather
Chinese-looking Mr. Lee, whom, because he came
from afar, Rachel rhymed with sea.

It wasn't exactly prize-winning stuff, but this was
Rachel writing, at the age of eight perhaps, of life as

she saw it and lived it on the Carson place. Mr. Lee was real, too. He ran a laundry down on Pittsburgh Street.

She knew the difference, however, between her own efforts and such poems as Colonel Thomas Wentworth Higginson's "The Soul of a Butterfly" in her *Jones Fourth Reader*:

> Over the field where the brown quails whistle
> Over the ferns where the rabbits lie,
> Floats the tremulous down of a thistle,
> Is it the soul of a butterfly?
>
> . . . .
>
> Come next August, when thistles blossom,
> See how each is alive with wings!
> Butterflies seek their souls in its bosom,
> Changed henceforth to immortal things.

What a discovery to make in a printed page. There were other people who looked with wondering eyes at the small creatures of the earth, who tried to understand the mystery of these unhuman lives—even experienced adults; even a soldier like Colonel Higginson, who had fought the fierce Confederates.

The colonel's poem may fall strangely on the ears of today's youth, but in its time it was a nice poem. It all seemed real to Rachel. There were no quail on the Carson place, but there were woodcocks, pheasants, and wild rabbits in the deep woods that began a few hundred yards beyond her house.

Once or twice Robert let Rachel come along with him when he went hunting. The woods were full of

small plants, birds, and insects she would have liked
to look at, but her head was full of Robert's instruc-
tions: "Walk close to me, on the side away from my
gun. Don't walk ahead of me. Keep in sight. Walk
slowly, quietly. Don't step on dry twigs."

"Like Indians?"

"That's right. Like Indians."

They would walk without talking much while
Robert's handsome Gordon setter, Don, prowled to
the left, to the right, and ahead of them, his dog-
footsteps rustling the dead leaves and the underbrush
as he went.

When Robert, once in a while, came home with a
rabbit he had shot, he was not applauded by the Carson womenfolk as a hero of field and forest. Though
Mrs. Carson would dress and cook the rabbit, she
would make it clear that she did not approve. She also
set an example of nonviolence toward nature by her
treatment of insects and spiders that infiltrated the
house. She put them outdoors instead of killing them.

There did come a time when young Rachel
plucked up courage to say something to her big
brother.

"Why do you shoot rabbits, Robert?"

"Hunting is fun. I don't shoot many."

"It can't be much fun for the rabbits. I think it's
better to watch them nibble things and see them
run."

It was Robert's recollection of the matter in later
years that "somewhere along the line I began to get
ashamed of myself. I'd walk up there and look at that

little rabbit lying there, still kicking. I'd ask myself what in the world I was doing this for. We didn't need them. And I really got ashamed of myself."

Evenings were family time. There was no television tube to beam its cold, steady glow at silent listeners hour after hour. There were no transistor radios to pour bad music after good into the ears of anyone old enough to flip a switch. And going to the movies was a few-and-far-between event. Most evenings, members of a family had to *be* with each other whether they liked it or not. They had to *talk* to each other and they had to make their own entertainment together.

A long day's work did not prevent Maria Carson from playing the piano and singing alto in the all-Carson home quintette. Robert, senior, would oblige once in a while with a solo rendition of "Oh, Dem Golden Slippers," "Carry Me Back to Old Virginny," or "Beautiful Ohio."

Reading out loud was a fairly common family pastime in Rachel's growing-up years. Mother read beautifully and enjoyed doing so. The children listened with their minds as well as with their ears . . . "Could you read just a little slower, Mother? . . . Would you mind reading that last part again?"

Summer and winter the Carson cellar was well stored with apples bedded in straw—Roman Beauties, russets, English Rambeaus, pippins, and other varieties from their orchard. Much of Mrs. Carson's performance was accompanied by the cheery crunch of apples being eaten by her listeners. They would pluck them out of the big bowl on the dining room table without taking their eyes off her.

They never ran out of apples or books; and mama never ran out of breath. One evening, however, they tired her completely. While reading *The Last of the Mohicans* she fell asleep in the middle of a sentence, murmuring "as close to the shore as possible . . ." Rachel and the others giggled and roused their mother, and everyone called it a night. The phrase "as close to the shore as possible" became a treasured bit of humorous family lore.

These evening sessions stirred a book-hunger in Rachel that she began to satisfy by independent reading even as a first- and second-grader. She delighted in the animal stories written and illustrated by Beatrix Potter, an Englishwoman. She enjoyed reading about Peter Rabbit, who lost his shoe while raiding a carrot patch; about Tabitha Twitchet, who kept a store and criticized another cat for being friendly with dogs; and about Pickles, a terrier, who worried because he didn't have the money to renew his dog license.

Miss Potter's books were more than juvenile entertainment for Rachel. They were a mirror of her feelings about the fields and woods, about the small creatures, tame and wild, who were part of her personal world—of her environment. They were vague, wordless feelings, the uncertain workings of a small girl's mind turned on by the first glimmerings of an idea that there may be some great mysterious unity in

all of nature; that everything in the world may somehow be connected with everything else.

In common with thousands of schoolgirls of her
generation, Rachel discovered *Freckles,* a book by
Gene Stratton Porter. The hero is a red-haired teen-
age orphan, one-handed as the result of a childhood
tragedy. He runs away from the Chicago orphans'
home where he has grown up and finds a job in a
Michigan lumber camp. Patrolling 2,000 acres of
rich forest land, he walks fourteen miles of boundary
fences daily in sub-zero weather, overcomes a vil-
lainous lumber thief in a rough-and-tumble fight,
saves the life of the boss's daughter who has earlier
saved his life, falls in love with her, discovers he is the
long-lost son of a titled Irishman, marries the girl,
and lives happily ever after.

It was not merely the action and romance that
stirred young Rachel. She was equally moved by the
author's portrayal of Freckles' uneducated but intelligent love of nature. She thrilled with sympathy at
the scene in which the lonely boy watches a Luna
moth wriggle out of its cocoon, and marveling at its
size and shape and color, cries out: "I don't know
what it is! Oh, how I wish I knew! How I wish I
knew! It must be something grand. It can't be a butterfly! It's a way too big. Oh, I wish there were someone to tell me what it is!"

With or without apples, Rachel's appetite for the
printed word continued to grow. By the time she was
ten and in the fourth grade she was sure she wanted to
be a professional writer. Reading *St. Nicholas,* the

leading children's magazine of the era, made her doubly sure. Its glossy pages were filled with articles, photographs, short stories, "continued" stories, drawings, poetry, puzzles, games. For tens of thousands of children and teen-agers, the day they got their hands on the new issue was the biggest day of the month.

What made *St. Nicholas* remarkable was that it sincerely respected the intelligence of its young readers. It invited them to send original writings and pictures to a special department called The St. Nicholas League. The best among the hundreds that came to the editors each month were published, but all of the senders became League members. The published pieces bore the authors' by-lines and ages. There were rather generous cash payments and a system of honor awards. In later decades many of these young contributors became famous as writers—among them Stephen Vincent Benét, Babette Deutsch, Eudora Welty, and Sterling North. Long after the magazine went out of business in the 1930's The St. Nicholas League continued to be remembered as a nursery of budding talents.

Rachel never doubted that she could do as well as any of the League authors, or better. Her first opportunity resulted from the explosion of a world event that made itself felt even in Springdale. The year was 1917. The United States, after trying to keep out of World War I for almost three years, was getting ready to fight overseas. Robert, eighteen, who had wanted to study electrical engineering, joined the U.S. Army Aviation Service instead. His training experiences in Texas gave Rachel a timely subject. When her story was finished she showed it to her mother, who read it studiously and said, "It seems quite good to me."

Rachel mailed it and waited for something to happen. Issue after issue of *St. Nicholas* arrived. She read each one with enjoyment, as though she felt no disappointment at not finding her own story in it. She was particularly interested in the nature articles: "The Sea-Otter, an Animal That Is Rapidly Becoming Extinct"; "Luminous Plants" (which glow at night); "The Burning Mine of Pennsylvania" (whose coal had smouldered underground for sixty-eight years, defying all efforts to put the fire out).

Her patience was rewarded by the September 1918 issue. She turned to The St. Nicholas League pages, and there it was:

A BATTLE IN THE CLOUDS
By Rachel L. Carson (Age 10)
(SILVER BADGE)

This is a story about a famous aviator who was in the Royal Flying Corps until he was killed in this country instructing other men. The main facts of this story were told to me by my brother, who is a soldier. The aviator had been several years in France. One day, when he and one of his companions were flying, a German plane suddenly burst upon them from behind a cloud. The two planes began firing, and the anti-aircraft guns of the Allies and Germans began firing. For a while, neither

plane was injured, but soon . . . a part of one wing
of the Canadian aviator's plane had been shot away.
The plane wavered, and he knew that if something
was not done promptly, the plane would fall. He
saw there was only one thing to do, and he did it
quickly. He crawled out along the wing, inch by
inch, until he reached the end. He then hung from
the end of the wing, his weight making the plane
balance properly. The Germans saw him but could
not but respect and admire the daring and courage
of the aviator, and did not fire until the plane
landed safely. The aviator was killed a few months
ago in a training camp in this country, and, in my
opinion, the Allies, by his death, lost a brave and
daring soldier.

There was something else in the mail that month
—a letter from *St. Nicholas* containing a check for
ten dollars, which was pretty serious money in those
days. To be published *and* paid stirred more excitement in Rachel than she allowed herself to show out-
wardly. If grown-ups or teachers at school said, "That
was a very nice story," or "I saw your story in *St.
Nicholas,*" she just smiled her quiet little smile and
said "Thank you," as if the whole thing didn't matter
much. Secretly, she could hardly wait to try again.
She just *had* to. Otherwise she would never know
how much of this first success was plain old luck and
how much of it was her own real ability. *St. Nicholas*
for February 1919 told her what she wanted to know
by publishing "A Message to the Front," by Rachel L.

Carson, Age 11, Gold Badge. It sounded more or less like the little essays hundreds of thousands of other children were writing in their classrooms about the importance of buying Liberty Bonds, except that it was so well written:

> Deep down in a dugout several French officers were sitting. There had been hard fighting for some time, and the officers were having an important meeting to discuss the next attack.
>
> It was a dark night, and a light rain was falling. The shells were bursting everywhere, and the cannon were firing incessantly.
>
> Suddenly a messenger appeared at the door. He was breathless from running. He was covered with mud and bleeding with wounds. "A message, sir," he said, halting in the doorway and saluting. He handed the officer a paper.
>
> The officer took it and read it without a word. Then he rose and said, "Gentlemen, America has drawn her sword." That was all, but, oh, how much those few words meant to France! . . .

The publication of the second story meant much to Rachel. On the printed page it seemed fresh and new, as though it had been written by some other Rachel L. Carson she had never met but of whose work she approved.

A third piece—"A Famous Sea-Fight," by Rachel L. Carson, Age 11, Honor Member—was printed in the August 1919 issue. It was a short account of Admiral Dewey's famous victory over the enemy's fleet at Manila Bay in the Spanish-American War. *St. Nicholas* had published three of Rachel's stories in twelve months. In her mind it was no longer a matter of what she wanted to be but of what she was *going* to be.

Young Rachel's achievement gave deep and private comfort to her mother. The rehearsed harmonies of the Washington Quintette and the hesitant tinkling of the tunes she used to invent, alone at the parlor piano, continued to occupy a corner of Maria Carson's mind long after her marriage. Four years before Rachel was born, Mrs. Carson had composed a musical setting for some light verse by Mary Mapes Dodge, the editor of *St. Nicholas,* and had mailed it to the magazine. In due course she received a reply from the associate editor:

"Dear Madam: Mrs. Dodge requests us to say that she thinks your setting to her little verses, 'Going to London,' a charming bit of music, and *St. Nicholas* will pay five dollars for it, for use in the magazine. With her thanks also for your very hearty and welcome letter . . . ."

Now, though she could hardly remember the music, Maria Carson remembered the letter sharply. It made her more determined than ever that Rachel should get the chance to be whatever Rachel wanted to be.

GROWING . . . GROWING . . . GROWN!

The business of America is business.

—CALVIN COOLIDGE

. . . Progress is a comfortable disease . . . .

—E. E. CUMMINGS

All of America, including Springdale, was Progress-happy during the first thirty years of the twentieth century.

Progress meant a better chance for people to live healthier, better-educated, longer lives than earlier generations had enjoyed. It also meant automobiles and gasoline instead of horses and oats; highways instead of wagon roads; telephones instead of penny postcards. It meant faster trains, airplanes, submarines, pianos that played themselves, phonographs, movies, radios. Progress was more people moving to cities while fewer people produced bigger crops on farms, with the help of modern machinery and chemical fertilizers. It meant digging more coal and iron, pumping more oil out of the ground, chop-

29

ping down more trees in the forests, dragging more fish out of the oceans.

It was understood, of course, that science played an important role in all of this, though most people did not really know how or why. In the popular thinking of these years science was a sort of educated magic for making the natural world do whatever human beings wanted it to do.

Most of all, Progress was an idea that kept Americans in a state of hopeful excitement, even those who couldn't pay their rent. Very few persons thought of asking "progress toward *what?*" because the answer seemed so ridiculously clear. America was moving toward a future of more, bigger, and better Everything.

Springdale itself was not exactly at the head of the big Progress parade, but it kept pace as well as a small town could. Its population increased from 1,199 in 1910 to 2,929 in 1920. The Franklin glue factory, which had been the only one within 600 miles, was replaced during Rachel's girlhood years by a generating plant of the West Penn Power Company. There was also a glass factory that used sand gouged out of the Moyer property bordering the Carsons'. Along Pittsburgh Street there were streetcar tracks, stores, saloons, business offices, two banks, and several churches.

It could well have been this rosy vision of twentieth-century progress that brought Robert W. Carson to Springdale. Exactly what he planned to do with his sixty-five acres was not entirely clear. Time would take care of that. Progress, in the form of mills, factories, mines, was moving up the Allegheny Valley from Pittsburgh—to say nothing of people who were finding "the Smoky City" just too unattractive to live in. All he had to do was wait. In five, ten—fifteen years at most—rising prices of land could make him very prosperous indeed. Meanwhile his holdings gave him what land always gives to its owners—a homeplace, a sense of independence, and respectful treatment by bank officials. The more so since he had acquired ten additional acres.

While he was waiting, Rachel's father engaged in other real-estate transactions, sold insurance, and earned wages as an electrical substation operator for the power company. He stuck to his plans to divide his property into building lots, however, because that's where the *real* money would come from. It didn't.

Progress, moving so fast that it tripped over its own feet, stumbled into periods of economic depression in 1907, 1913, and in the years just after World War I. Nor did epidemics of polio in 1916, and influenza in 1918 and 1920, put people in a mood to buy building lots. Worse, the hard-fought strikes which gusted through the Allegheny Valley's railroad, steel, and coal industries made very unhealthy weather for the real-estate business.

Carson found that he couldn't sell the building lots all at once and put his "winnings" into bigger and better ventures, as he had sometimes hoped. Instead he had to sell one lot at a time, when he could get a fair price. He also used his land as security to borrow money from the bank when he needed it, which he often did.

"He would come in and have to get some money once in a while," a Springdale bank employee of those days recalled. "He was sometimes slow in payment but the bank never lost any money on him, of course. He had enough real estate to back all of his borrowings."

The fact is that Progress never kept more than a small part of its fat financial promise to Robert W. Carson. His land did increase in value but only enough to keep his family decently provided for. He was respected around town as a man of dignified bearing who always wore white shirts, even on weekdays—a quiet man but one who "when he said something, he knew what it meant." Many of the townspeople thought him aloof, but to another local banking official he seemed to be "a man who was easily approached." As a businessman, Robert W. Carson plainly lacked "the killer instinct." He didn't have the heart to charge more than fifty cents a bushel for the choice apples Springdale residents bought from him on a pick-'em-yourself basis. Nor was he especially ferocious with the young immigrant glass-factory workers who came from the company-owned houses near the river to carry away apples by the sackful on a steal-'em-yourself basis. He would sternly order them to leave, not because they were taking his apples, but because they were hurting the trees by throwing clubs at the branches to jar the fruit loose.

He was not so easily approached, however, by a coal-mining company that wanted to pay him for the right to extend its tunnels under his land from points outside of Springdale. The offer was attractive because it meant good, hard ready cash. But it wasn't enough to make him run the risk of hurting his subdivision plan. Who would want to buy building lots on top of a coal-mining tunnel? Suppose the surface caved in? That happened sometimes.

It is quite likely that his refusal did not really protect his land. He was sure that *somebody* was digging coal *somewhere* underneath his property, year after year, without his permission. It was easy enough for him to protect his orchard from penniless, policeman-shy, immigrant factory hands. It was something else to stop underground trespassing by a wealthy coal-mining company. It would have been terribly complicated and costly. So, Mr. Carson did nothing about it. He went about his business feeling deep twinges of chagrin now and then, like an ex-soldier whose old wounds act up on rainy days.

A sharp operator might have taken the coal company's money and sold his lots, too. But it just wasn't in Robert Carson's makeup to sell real estate while muttering under his breath, "Let the buyer beware." There weren't many buyers anyway.

"Property didn't move too fast at that period," one of the local bank men recalled. "Mr. Carson was what you might call real-estate-poor, because it wasn't selling well, or real-estate-rich, because he had so much of it."

In practical terms, it came down to this: The Carsons were modestly comfortable. They never lacked good food, proper clothing, good medical attention, books, newspapers, magazines, music, a horse and buggy and, later, an automobile. Nevertheless, Rachel's brother recalled that "there was something of an impression around town that we were rolling in money. It bothered us because it was the kind of false impression that's hard to correct."

The elder Carson's disappointment about the year-to-year improvement of his real-estate investment was not allowed to weigh heavily on the minds of his children. For Rachel, daily life was enjoyably crowded with chores, school, homework, reading of her own choice, and simply being outdoors.

She was not without the company of girls her own age, though she lived on the outskirts of town. But she did not make friends readily or carelessly. This was an attitude her mother encouraged. It was an attitude that confirmed Springdale's judgment that the Carsons were "a little choicy in their associations, somewhat withdrawn, and didn't encourage visiting to any extent." Certainly the girls who did become the companions of Rachel's grammar-school and high-school years felt they were subject to Mrs. Carson's approval, but those who won it valued it.

Irene Mills was one of the chosen few. Rachel's

father or brother would call for Irene in a horse and buggy on Saturday mornings and bring her home again early in the evening after supper. When the weather kept them indoors the two girls were content with dolls, cutout books, and games—a rubber ball and jacks on the back porch or Parcheesi in the parlor. When they were older there were magazines, books, and the piano as entertainment resources. But Rachel liked to be off and running about the Carson acres whenever Irene and the weather were willing. There was always something new to see, something familiar to rediscover.

Though the two girls had a strong sympathy for each other, Irene felt that Rachel was basically a "loner." There seemed to be an invisible line in their girlish intimacy that Rachel never invited her friend to cross. Nevertheless, Irene enjoyed her visits. "There was always something to *do* there."

Charlotte Fisher, somewhat younger than Rachel, liked walking through the Carsons' woods on Sunday afternoons. Stopping at their house, she was always welcomed cordially. Over tea, cookies, and apples, there were lively conversations, usually led by Rachel's mother, about events and ideas of the time. All three were eager to tell each other about the books they had been reading. Springdale had no public library then. Charlotte, who made frequent trips to a Pittsburgh library, brought back books for the Carsons and borrowed books from them. She remembered the relationship in later years as being based "not on dates or on being in the same crowd but as an intellectual kind of friendship with highly civilized people."

There was at least one girlhood crowd that Charlotte and Rachel did have in common—the eight children of Dr. Herman E. Krumpe, a dentist. Mildred Krumpe and Rachel developed a strong mutual sympathy in their grammar-school years. In the Krumpes' huge back yard, which often looked and sounded like Saturday afternoons at a small county fair, Rachel and Mildred kept close to each other. Both were quiet, bookish, unathletic. They preferred to remain at the edge of the action, which included picnic lunches on the grass, swings, croquet, and rides on the Krumpes' two Shetland ponies, Bill and Betty. They joined the juvenile hurly-burly of fun and games when talk about their own special interests lagged or when the spirit moved them. Both were quick, however, to fall in with any cluster that formed for group singing at the parlor piano.

Rachel's teachers, understandably, took greater notice of her than most of her classmates did. Minerva Baker, assistant principal at Springdale High School, regarded her as a very unusual child. She was impressed with some of Rachel's compositions. She read them at a teachers' meeting, not because of their technical quality but because they showed remarkable depth of thought and feeling.

Mrs. Baker also cherished the fact that Rachel, given a dressmaking assignment in her home economics class, turned in not only a very creditable garment but a hat to match. Rachel, however, was less interested in clothes for their own sake than most high school girls. Neither she nor her mother haunted the Pittsburgh department stores in search of "the latest thing." The Carsons were content with Springdale's verdict that they managed to be "very nice-looking in an unpretentious way."

Rachel came to the parting of ways with the Krumpe children, Charlotte Fisher, and other childhood friends when she was sixteen because Springdale High was a two-year school then. Many Springdale students chose to transfer to Peabody High in East Liberty. That meant a 35-minute ride on the Conemaugh Division of the Pennsylvania Railroad. Rachel settled for Parnassus High School in New Kensington, a mere two streetcar miles from home. Aside from saving time and railroad fare, it didn't matter. She had made a two-year average grade of 93.7 at Springdale High. In her following two years at Parnassus she did almost equally well, with an average of 93.5. She was just two days past her eighteenth birthday when she walked up the auditorium aisle to receive her diploma.

It was an unsettling moment, part joyous, part solemn, and just a touch frightening. A rush of ideas, questions, and feelings came tumbling through her mind, powerfully, like the springtime Allegheny swollen to flood level . . . I've got a diploma . . . What now? . . . What now?

On the way out, after the commencement exercise, a few classmates stopped her to say goodbye. There were the usual leave-taking rituals. They signed each other's autograph albums, said "good luck," and talked about their plans for the immediate future.

Where was Rachel going in the fall? Pennsylvania College for Women in Pittsburgh, she replied. One girl pretended to be envious because Rachel would be so close to Pittsburgh University and Carnegie Tech, where boys would abound. Rachel, no amusement showing in her grey-blue eyes, stared the girl down.

"My major is going to be literature, not boys."

THE GIRL FROM SPRINGDALE

Filiae nostrae sicut antarii lapides
[*That our daughters may be as the polished cornerstones of palaces*].

— MOTTO OF CHATHAM COLLEGE

September was half over. Her bags were packed. She
was ready to go. There was still time, though, to look
around, and look back. Standing near the fireplace in
the parlor, she stared at the big conch shell on the
mantelpiece, trying to remember the first time she
had seen it . . .

When she was very little someone told her she
could "hear the ocean" by putting the shell to her ear.
She did, believingly, and was rewarded by a fascinating sound—a slow, hollow hissing that grew
stronger, then fainter, as though with the beat of her
own heart. Every once in a while in the years that followed, she tried it again. Then she would turn the
shell over in her hand and look intently at its delicate
pink and dazzling white mouth. And one day she
knew—it was not the sound of the ocean but the
great mystery of the ocean's existence that remained
in the shell. She had never seen the animal that lived
in it. But she read hints of vast and hidden wonders in

39

the shell—the clever cone-shaped way it curled into itself; the hard yet silky smoothness on the inner side of its flaring lip; the whole shell's compact weight as her fingers closed on the polished bumpiness of its outer surfaces . . .

And now it seemed to her that there had never been a time when she had not thought or dreamed or wondered about the sea, though she had never seen it . . . She reached for the conch, held it to her ear for a moment, and put it down again, secretly smiling. The sea! Well, someday . . . for sure . . . all in good time. Then she went into the kitchen to find her mother. They walked down the front steps together. The family automobile was parked at the curb. Her luggage was neatly stowed and Father was waiting in the driver's seat.

Pennsylvania College for Women, which changed its name to Chatham College in 1955, was part of the city of Pittsburgh but apart from it. The school sat on a high bluff north and somewhat east of the business district, a sort of collegiate island in the Pittsburgh sky. From the edge of the campus one could look across a vista of treetops that gave aerial camouflage to the attractive residential streets and broad avenues directly below. Seen through the carbon curtain of the city's factory fog, more distant points were doubtful actualities.

Away from their brink, the campus acres rolled across long grassy slopes, broad tended lawns, and wooded knolls. There were flower beds in angles

sheltered by the buildings. Trees were everywhere
—elms, maples, beeches, oaks—the kind whose
cultivated size and symmetry mark the places where
higher learning is pursued. In the half century since
Chatham's beginning, its trees had grown statelier,
the turf of its lawns deeper and springier; the ivy
thicker on the walls of Berry, Dilworth, and Wood-
land Halls.

There were more compelling considerations in the
choosing of Rachel's college. The small size of the
student body, about three hundred, offered the kind
of campus environment Mrs. Carson favored. The
impressive bearing of Chatham's president, Cora
Helen Coolidge, suggested that the school's academic
standards were what Mrs. Carson thought they ought
to be. What's more, Chatham was close to home. And
a notation in the catalog made it even closer: "A few
scholarships are open to students who . . . need
financial aid in meeting the necessary expenses of a
college education." Well, Rachel certainly did. The
sale of Father's lots, one by one, was still enough to
keep the Carson household economically afloat. But
the family could hardly stand the additional strain of
$1,000 a year for tuition, books, lab fees, room,
board, and unpredictable *et ceteras*.

Scholarships were small and few in the 1920's.
Since Chatham was able to grant Rachel only $100 a
year from its own funds, Cora Coolidge and Dean
Mary Marks took additional steps. They got some
well-to-do personal friends to help, unofficially and
very privately.

Rachel did not seem to need any time for adjustment to the college classroom. Surprise quizzes that caught her fellow students flat-footed found Rachel on her toes and scoring high. She even managed to earn B-plus in violin, for her required freshman music course. By the end of the fall 1925 semester, Misses Coolidge and Marks knew they had picked a winner. The shy, businesslike girl from Springdale was one of the ten highest-ranking freshmen in the school.

In the "roaring '20's," when most Americans were busy chasing all sorts of rainbows for fun and profit, this kind of excellence was not readily forgiven by average students anywhere. The national mood made it easy for them to feel that they must not let their studies interfere too seriously with more entertaining activities. Many of Chatham's young ladies came from prosperous homes. They wore fashionable "college clothes," spent their allowances girlishly, looked forward to dates, proms, informal dances, and holidays. They did their homework and respected the school regulations but they didn't believe in overdoing it. Only a few had their minds firmly made up to follow careers of their own— marriage or no marriage.

It was perfectly possible, of course, for a brainy freshman to be popular with her classmates, if she took the trouble. Rachel, whether she thought about the matter or not, didn't bother.

So, what was the matter with Rachel? The others wondered, shrugged, then let her go her own way.

Why worry forever about a girl who was so *different*? If she wanted to spend her weekends in the library and in her room at Berry Hall studying and writing . . . Oh well, that was *her* business. But what, for pity's sake, was she writing about? Nobody could have *that* many themes, reports, term papers, and what-all.

To classmates who lived in the same dorm and attended the same classes, the girl was no puzzle, though she seldom talked about herself. They drew intelligent conclusions on which half a dozen of them could readily agree, and which one of them put into clear-cut words many years later: "She wasn't anti-social. She just wasn't social. Being poor had some bearing on that. She didn't have the clothes or the extra things a girl needed at college then. And Rachel did have to accept financial help, which was more of a stigma in those days than later."

On the other hand, Mary Kolb, another classmate, remembered: "Though she was much more of a scholar than the rest of us and in a way withdrawn, she entered into things with great spirit. When you asked her to do something, she did it wholeheartedly —if she wanted to do it."

Looked at a little sideways by some of the girls, treated with indifference by most of them, Rachel seemed to need no one's good opinion except her own. Her manner was friendly though not warm. She was soft-spoken but not meek. She knew how to deal with anyone who tried "to step on what she considered to be her rights." On the other hand, she never put on airs about her superior abilities as a student. All she ever expected was to be allowed to follow her own interests in her own way.

Coming nowhere near popularity, Rachel was nevertheless respected—a little grudgingly in her first two years, more wholeheartedly later on. As a freshman she tried out, not very successfully, for her class intramural basketball team.

Classmate Margaret Wooldridge recalled: "Rachel was a perennial substitute on the intramural hockey, baseball, and basketball teams. She was eligible because she attended enough practice sessions, but those first two years she wasn't quite good enough to make a regular place on the team."

She was more than good enough to become a reporter on the semimonthly student paper, *The Arrow*. Just before the end of her freshman year, the paper's special literary supplement, *Englicode,* published Rachel's lengthy short story, "The Master of the Ship's Light." It centered on the misunderstanding, separation, and final reconciliation of two friends who had worked together to design a new kind of lighthouse. Judged by professional standards the plot was awkwardly contrived and the characters poorly drawn. Yet the story had a strangely moving quality because of its setting, a seacoast "where the rugged bulk of Cape Arrowhead, a queer misshapen nose of granite, juts out into the waters."

The people were secondary. They were Rachel's excuse for writing about the sea; for trying to put into words the endless fascination that literature, music, and the surging sounds of the conch shell on the mantelpiece had kept alive in her through all her growing years. And what she wrote of the sea rang true, though she had not yet seen the immensity of its surfaces or shores:

> The coast was less hospitable than the people who inhabited it. Over the surface of the long lazy swells that rolled in on the shallow beach, played dark formless shadows or patches of white foam, betraying the menacing reefs beneath. When the icy winds swept down from the Straits, towering waves beat upon the coast with uncontrollable fury, and the booming of the breakers resounded for miles . . . .
> Huntleigh went slowly up the stairs. The wind, strengthened to a gale, beat furiously upon the house. A thousand fiendish voices joined in the fearful chorus. Stephen Huntleigh heard, and shuddered . . . .

In her sophomore year she held the undistinguished job of alumnae-news reporter on *The Arrow*. The *Englicode* issues, however, gave her opportunities to choose her own subjects. In a mini-story titled "Why I Am a Pessimist," she wrote:

> Who wouldn't be if they were in my place? . . . No one in this household pays any attention to me. Not that I can't get along without them well enough but it's the principle of the thing . . . .

The speaker turns out to be a cat who wants equal rights as a member of a human household. He complains that he is ordered about, deprived of his independence, and slighted in a dozen ways.

> . . . The family keeps bothering me about little details that don't matter. If I'm not good enough for them to talk to and associate with, I'm not good enough to torment, either . . . . They just don't get my viewpoint . . . . Some day I'm going away to live with a nice old lady who hasn't any other cats. She'll believe in a cat's right to be independent, and as good as anyone else. Then won't I come back here at night and howl on the fence! Won't I though!

The details of the cat's "personality" came from Rachel's long familiarity with such pets back in Springdale. But—and it's an old question—is there any writer who is not, somehow, writing about himself? Was "The Ugly Duckling" a story just about a bird? Or was it also about the awkward lonely boyhood of its author, Hans Christian Andersen? Was Rachel writing about her relations with her schoolmates? One guess is as good as another. There is no doubt, however, that this was an early example of the young, not-yet writer's mind at work. She was trying to use her personal experience and feeling to make statements about life, which her readers would recognize as true whether it pleased them or not. This,

really, is what all writers do. Those who do it successfully have mastered writing as an art.

As a sophomore, Rachel wrote about herself directly in a somewhat more sophisticated piece,
"Keeping an Expense Account." If the cat story was a
protest, this one was an undergraduate declaration of
independence:

> . . . To keep a careful account of one's finances,
> they tell you, is excellent training. I've tried it
> . . . . It's too hard on my nerves and my room-
> mate's . . . . Semi-monthly I balance my accounts
> . . . . Usually I've spent more than I can account
> for. But what a triumph if I (actually) have even ten
> cents which, by mathematical proof, I have long
> since spent, and therefore (supposedly) have not.
> Full of an unholy joy, I go out and spend the dime
> on a soda. For once I have got the better of that
> smug little black book. Yes, I'm through with ex-
> pense accounts . . . my little black book is going
> into the waste basket, never to return!

From issue to issue, the *Englicode* stories by
Rachel L. Carson grew more ambitious in subject
matter and style. Each one edged a little closer to professional quality. "The Golden Apple" was her
humorous retelling of the Greek myth about the
"beauty contest" on Mount Olympus. The myth in
its original form is simple enough. Eris, the trouble-
making goddess of discord, decides to break up a
wedding feast to which she has not been invited. She

throws a golden apple marked "for the fairest" into the banquet hall, and each of the three most powerful goddesses claims it. To settle their dispute they call on Paris, a prince of Troy. Juno, queen of the gods, promises to make him lord of Europe and Asia. Minerva, goddess of war and wisdom, says she will cause him to lead an army to victory over the Greeks and to bring their cities to ruin. But Paris, being a weakling and a little chickenhearted, turns away from these guarantees of power and glory. He hands the apple to Venus because she offers him Helen, the world's most beautiful woman. But Helen happens to be the wife of Menelaus of Troy. This judgment of Paris and his seizure of Helen, his promised reward, sets off the tragic war between Trojans and Greeks.

Rachel's version gave the ancient legend a certain fresh, up-to-date quality. At the same time, her own feelings were easy to find in the tone and coloring of her story. She sympathized with these divine females for having to submit to the decision of Paris, who admittedly didn't amount to much. She also thought they were ridiculous for doing so. And she found herself forced to agree with Venus that Paris could not be very different from most men, past or present, ancient or modern:

> . . . Venus looked at Paris . . . . She knew men. Paris would choose her, of course. She looked into his eyes and smiled. "Come now, Paris," she laughed. "What does any man want most of all? The

most beautiful woman in the world for his wife, of
course. I will give her to you."

Paris held up the golden apple by its glittering
stem . . . The most beautiful woman in the world
. . . He tossed the apple lightly into Venus' waiting hands.

"You win."

The choice between Minerva and Venus, so easily
made by Paris, was a choice that real life was also
forcing on Rachel. For her it was a complicated and
agonizing one. To the protectress she chose, she
would have to hand over not merely a golden apple
but herself and her future. She would have preferred
to go through life calling freely on Minerva's courage
and wisdom, without turning away from Venus'
power. She knew, however, that she was better made
to follow the stern goddess in armor than the tender
one draped in swirls of gauze. If she suffered from any
conflict between what she thought herself to be and
what she might wish to be, she kept it strictly to herself. Yet Rachel gave clear hints of such an inner
struggle in a 4,000-word short story, "Broken
Lamps."

The hero, Neil Sutherland, is an engineer who
dreams of designing a perfect bridge. It is to be a design in which neither the greatest strength nor the
greatest beauty will be sacrificed, one for the other.
He is unhappy because his wife, Joan, seems not to
understand his dream and his desperate need to make

it real. His unhappiness deepens until Joan's sudden illness causes him to open his eyes to "the truth." The perfect unity of strength and beauty that he is struggling to create, so unsuccessfully, already exists, not in a steel-and-stone bridge but in a flesh-and-blood human being, Joan herself.

"Broken Lamps" gave Rachel a blaze of glory in which to end her sophomore year. It won the annual prize offered by Omega, the campus English club. It appeared in the *Englicode* issue of May 27, 1927, the date of her twentieth birthday.

THE YEAR OF THE GOAT

When land is gone and money spent,
Then learning is most excellent.

—OLD ENGLISH RHYME

It was a common notion of the time that art and science were somehow hostile to each other. Science was respected because it enabled people to invent machines, cure diseases, and grow bigger crops. At the same time it was also resentfully accused of taking the beauty and the mystery out of things—the rainbow's arch or the birds' flight—by explaining them in precise, cold-blooded language.

Rachel preferred the poet's point of view. Nevertheless, since Chatham girls needed two semesters of science credit for graduation, she enrolled as a sophomore in biology 1 and 2. What she lacked in enthusiasm for the subject, she made up in curiosity about the teacher. Any science course taught by Mary Scott Skinker was worth taking, if one could stand the pace.

Mary Skinker was thirty-four, small-featured, genuinely pretty. Dark hair piled high on her head made her seem somewhat taller than medium height. The salient feature of her subtly molded face was a generous mouth that curved upward, ready to smile.

White dresses, graceful carriage, and a certain far-away look gave her a wraithlike quality. Her undergraduate followers sometimes briefed newer students:

"If she walks by you without saying hello, don't think she's an awful snob. She's not, really. It's just that she's very nearsighted and doesn't wear glasses. If you speak to her first she'll recognize your voice and she'll answer."

Rachel soon discovered that biology, as taught by Miss Skinker, was much more than a matter of dreary definitions and tiresome lab demonstrations. This woman's teaching was impassioned as well as precise. She demanded more than mere excellence from her students. She wanted them to feel and understand all they could about the awesome web of life in which they were bound alike with the gigantic whale and the one-celled protozoan. *Homo sapiens* had an obligation to know and understand for the very reason that he was *Homo sapiens,* Man the Knowing and the Wise. Accordingly Miss Skinker did all she could to turn on the intelligence of those females of the species who signed up for her courses. She never succeeded more completely than she did in Rachel Carson's case. Listening to Miss Skinker was a mind-expanding experience for Rachel. She not only absorbed some of the facts, language, and method of biology; she began to recognize its meaning. It was a key to man's understanding of his remarkable and promising existence on earth. She discovered that the popularly imagined conflict between art and science seemed not to exist, after all. They were two equally important ways to see and know the natural world. What she learned that year helped her see nature not less lovingly but more sharply than she had ever seen it with her unaided poetic eye.

Rachel returned to Chatham for her junior year with doubts about keeping English as her major course of study. Not that she was less interested in writing; she was more interested in science. Zoology, physiology, and organic chemistry made up half of her third-year program. She never averaged less than an A-minus in these. At the same time she remained a "star" in the English courses of Professor Grace Croff, a dedicated teacher who had high literary hopes for Rachel.

During a study of standard poetic forms, Miss Croff assigned all hands to the writing of triolets, eight-line poems with a rather tricky rhyme scheme. Later she read selected samples of this homework to the class. For Betty MacColl, a classmate, it was a memorable session.

"We settled back to hear Miss Croff read the best of our creations. Most of them were really plodding. Then came this one:

> Butterfly poised on a thistle's down,
> Lend me your wings for a summer's day.
> What care I for a kingly crown,
> Butterfly poised on a thistle's down,
> When I might wear your gossamer gown,
> And sit enthroned on an orchid spray?

Butterfly poised on a thistle's down,
Lend me your wings for a summer's day!

"It was Rachel's, and the whole class fairly fell at her feet. 'How did you do it?' we asked. 'Well,' she said, 'I knew a triolet was supposed to be light, so I thought of the lightest things I could, a butterfly and thistle down.' She was a little embarrassed, possibly, for the rest of us who had been so inept."

Rachel had to cope quietly with a more familiar embarrassment—the same old shortage of funds. She was able to pay her annual $250 tuition by adding $150 to her $100 scholarship grant from Chatham. And for a time she managed not to fall too far behind in her payments for room, board, and laboratory fees. Nevertheless she would end her junior year owing the school $613.85. It was a sizeable sum but not big enough to worry Miss Coolidge. What did worry her and Dean Marks was the danger that Rachel might have to quit for lack of funds. They made sure that didn't happen. Rachel was equally determined. Work. Study. Get the best possible grades. Sooner or later there would be a way to wipe out her debt to Chatham. How she looked at life that year is easy to guess from a *hokku* she wrote as a poetry exercise for Miss Croff's specialized composition class.

The challenge of this traditional Japanese form is to create in exactly seventeen syllables a clear word-picture of a scene, action, or object, at the same time giving it a meaning greater than itself. Rachel's *hokku*, "Sumac," was a portrait of the hardy shrub

whose cone-shaped clusters of red berries remain on
its branches long after the trees around it have been
blown bare:

> Grim little Indian
> Grip tightly your swaying bough!
> Hold your painted cap!

Rachel, however, did not feel grim. Despite her
financial cares, life at Chatham had improved for
her. She was still a "loner," but two years of association had made her one of a handful of juniors and
seniors who shared the same campus interests. They
were English majors; staff members of *Arrow, Englicode,* or the college yearbook, *Pennsylvanian*; members of Omega; and hockey players.

Early in the year, Rachel established her position
as goalkeeper on the junior class intramural field-
hockey team. She played with a sureness she had not
shown during her first two years. A small, somewhat
chubby 115-pounder, there was nothing rugged
about Rachel. But opposing players who broke
through the backfield seldom got past her. She was
almost always where the action was, a split-second
ahead of the ball. Cool and dependable, she was considered "a whale of a goalie" by her teammates. It was
a whale of a team, too, by Chatham standards. It won
the 1927–28 school championship.

After the game Rachel would get out of her middy
blouse and gym bloomers, shower, dress, and go
about the more serious business of her school week.
Win or lose, the rest of the team usually piled into

someone's auto for a trip to Reymers', a constant *Arrow* advertiser ("Candies, Fountain Service. Meet Your Friends at Our East End Store. Cream and Ices Unequaled").

Repeatedly invited to go along, Rachel repeatedly refused. Once her classmate Margaret Wooldridge insisted. She remembered the brief conversation many years later:

"Come on. The whole gang's going over to Reymers'."

"Thanks, Peg. No. Some other time."

"Oh, come on, Rachel. It doesn't have to be expensive. Fifteen cents for a lime rickey. Lots of people do that."

Rachel shrugged as if to dismiss a completely unimportant matter. "Who's got fifteen cents?" And if that left the whole campus with the impression that she didn't have fifteen cents, so what? That was not the measure by which she judged other people.

When she chose to join the crowd, she was always welcome. And she did choose, when the crowd was doing her kind of thing. Late in February 1928 she wrote to Mary Frye, a science major who was her lab partner in Miss Skinker's invertebrate zoology course, and who was now in Florida recovering from an illness.

> Over the week-end there was a heavy snow. So we got up a coasting party and had a perfectly glorious time. The sky was absolutely clear with old Orion up over Miss Coolidge's house watching the fun.

We had two sleds and trays innumerable. We got the tray coasting down to a science. About ten we came in and had a hot and cold shower, then dressed in p.j.'s and bathrobes and went down to the drawing room. We lit a fire and I sat on the floor in front of it. We had potato salad, olives, sandwiches, and coffee. Then we turned off all the lights and sat there in the firelight and sang all the songs we knew until almost twelve. That was one of the nicest times I've had since I came to college. I wouldn't have missed it for anything.

Hockey games and sledding parties could never give her the excitement she experienced in the solitary effort of writing. Take the short play, for example, that appeared in the October 1927 *Englicode*. Its title, "Let's Raise Chickens," was not likely to inflame anyone's imagination. The script itself was strictly college-level amateur quality. Nevertheless, its tender, humorous understanding of two lonely people's need for each other made it a worthy piece of work.

The plot was simple. A middle-aged widow catches a bachelor who lives next door stealing her chickens but hides him from the constable who happens by. With the lawman gone, the widow's disapproval of her friendly neighborhood thief turns to sympathy. And the bachelor's pretended toughness crumbles. They decide that it is better for them to raise chickens together than for one to keep them or the other to steal them separately.

Nor could Rachel tell her teammates, in courtesy, about another preference. She would rather talk to Miss Skinker, to Mary Frye, and to Dorothy Thompson, another earnest science girl she had met in sophomore biology, than sit around at Reymer's. Despite the age and student-teacher differences, Rachel found herself on a footing of warm personal friendship with Miss Skinker.

They had much to talk about—literature and music as well as science. They discussed Rachel's growing doubts about wanting to be a professional writer and Mary Skinker's growing determination to work for her Ph.D. Occasionally they chatted about field trips, past or future. Miss Skinker liked to lead her students, and Rachel liked to go, to places where they could see biology actually happening. Sometimes they chose locations along the interurban railway between Pittsburgh and Butler, Pennsylvania, which ran through a region of forest, pools, and streams hemmed in by steeply rising cliffs. They hunted trailing arbutus and identified wild flowers, and once Rachel, exultant, recognized her first ovenbird.

Another time they went to Cook State Forest, a 6,000-acre wilderness that had somehow remained undamaged despite three centuries of white settlement. And at McConnell's Mill they explored the line where the glacier of the last Ice Age had stopped, leaving a fish fossil for Rachel to discover in the soft stone of a hillside.

Dissecting crayfish, starfish, grasshoppers, and

frogs, Rachel moved deeper into a new world of learning. She had entered it as a sort of intellectual tourist to see what she could see, but she decided to remain. She changed her course of major studies from English to science.

"I have something very exciting to tell you," she wrote to Mary Frye. "I've changed my major. To what? Biology, of course! All year I've been enjoying the people who were majoring in it. I finally decided to do it."

Mary Skinker was pleasantly astounded, but Miss Croff was dismayed. Even Chatham's president expressed grave doubts about the wisdom of Rachel's decision. Rachel, chagrined by this unexpected resistance, wrote to Mary Frye:

"Miss Coolidge, etc., have been kicking up a fine row about my schedule and my major in general . . . . The powers that be would just as leave there weren't any science majors."

Though most of her teachers were sympathetic to her choice, she wrote to Mary, "You ought to see the reactions I get. I've gotten bawled out and called all sorts of blankety-blank names so much that it's beginning to get monotonous. That's all from the other girls, of course . . . ."

It seemed to "the other girls" that Rachel was turning away from certain success as a writer to become nothing more than another obscure science teacher in some high school or women's college. Outside of teaching and a few government jobs, there were very few opportunities for women in science in the 1920's.

A woman biologist running her own laboratory and directing her own program of original research work was a rarity. Popular literature, on the other hand, was a rainbow career worth chasing, with honors and a pot of gold at the end—if a girl had talent and a little luck.

Rachel, the literature student, knew what Coleridge meant when he wrote: "He prayeth best who loveth best/All things both great and small." Rachel, the biology student, squinting through her microscope at the jewel-like skeleton of a radiolarian, pondered another truth—he loveth best who *knoweth* best. The trouble was that most people didn't know beans about biology or the other sciences. If they did they would be as fascinated as she was by the marvels, massive or microscopic, of the living world. They would understand the joy she found in climbing three long flights of nighttime-creaking stairs to the science lab in the tower of Dilworth Hall.

As for writing, why invent imaginary people and imaginary problems? Wasn't it better to investigate Life itself—how it starts and grows and keeps itself going and reproduces itself and dies—and starts and grows . . . Life, that wonderful continuous happening which happens alike to plankton and to presidents, to starfish and to movie stars.

"We can have a great time in some of those courses," she wrote to the still-absent Mary Frye. "Yesterday we had lots of fun dissecting *Amphioxus*. We're going to do the dog-fish next week . . . . The dog-fish is such fun. I wish we were doing it together.

They make your hands and books and everything smell awful, though . . . . Do bring back a Portuguese Man of War."

There was just too much to do and enjoy that spring. But she did find time for one "big" date— a rare occasion in her college years—on a weekend in March. She invited Bob Frye, no relation to Mary, to the Junior Prom. Frye, a junior at Westminster College, took her to a basketball game at his school, some fifty miles from Pittsburgh, the following day.

> Day after tomorrow is the Prom! [she wrote to Mary]. I'm wearing my silver slippers now hoping they won't hurt so much. [A week later she reported] Yes, I did have a glorious time . . . . It was so pretty. They had very dim lighting most of the time, and kept flashing green, lavender, and yellow lights across the room. A trifle hard on the eyes but indescribably pretty on the glass chandeliers and the mirror walls . . . . I had an awfully nice week-end . . . . Miss Skinker was a perfect knockout at the Prom. She wore peach-colored chiffon-velvet, with the skirt shirred just about 8 inches in front, and a rhinestone pin at the waist. Then she wore a choker necklace of rhinestones and two longer ones of tiny pearls.

She saw Bob Frye at least once more, the following month, though she had sufficient reason to postpone the date. Suffering from an abcessed tooth, she went home to Springdale for dental treatment on Saturday and stayed overnight, but returned to Chatham early on Sunday to meet him.

Her senior year, beginning in September 1928, left her no time and little inclination for dates. There were six science courses on her schedule. She would have to get top marks—and to her usual motivation was added a wish to prove that she had not been mistaken in changing her major course of study. She shouldered her work load eagerly, though a little less joyously than she might have. Mary Skinker was taking a leave of absence to study for her Ph.D. at Johns Hopkins University. Classroom and lab—indeed, the whole campus—seemed incomplete without her. Rachel missed her sorely, not merely as an instructress but as the person who had inspired her still-growing excitement about science. They wrote to each other once in a while. Rachel was a little saddened to learn that her teacher had become too ill to go on with her doctoral work. But Miss Skinker, living with an elder sister in Washington, continued to write cheerful, engaging letters.

When she was not otherwise occupied, Rachel grappled with the ghostly arithmetic of getting through her senior year on money she didn't have. She had earned $75 during the summer tutoring two high school students in geometry, Latin, and English. This plus $100 scraped from somewhere near the bottom of the family barrel got her past the front door. The rest would have to be a matter of Chatham's patience and Rachel's fortitude.

Mostly, she was too busy to worry about it. She had science on her mind—histology, genetics, chemistry, and a required two-semester seminar for biology majors. She also took on a year of German, following two years of French and a year of Italian.

It was her busiest season in all-around student activity, too. She was proofreader for *The Arrow,* a job of particular importance on any student newspaper. Somewhat to her own amazement, she was elected president of the new science club she, Mary Frye, and Dorothy Thompson had taken the lead in organizing. It was named Mu Sigma—M. S. in the Greek alphabet—for Mary Skinker.

Most of Rachel's class, however, would remember 1928 as the year of the goat. For the first time, the best hockey players from each of the four class hockey teams were chosen to form two honorary "all-star" teams. These promptly dubbed themselves Army and Navy and prepared to play for the college championship. It would hardly have been television material even in those days, but it was the big event of the school's athletic year.

Rachel, Navy's goalkeeper, was around when Captain Mary Kolb called a short meeting of the team at the end of a practice session. Since this was to be an "Army-Navy" game, Mary thought it would add excitement if the team were to show up on the field with the traditional Navy mascot, a goat. There was enthusiastic agreement but—where could they get one and who would get it? Rachel volunteered.

She never confided the details of the transaction to her teammates. But on the day of the big game she delivered *two* goats to the campus, a nanny and her inseparable kid. Near the hockey field she handed the leash rope to Betty MacColl, Navy's official goat keeper for the day. A tug-of-war followed immediately. Tiring, Betty tried to tie her end of the rope to a small tree. Before she knew it, the goat had run circles around her, lashing her securely to the trunk.

Rachel, choking down her laughter, came to the rescue. Between halves, the goat dragged Betty face down along the field, and for an encore, butted one of the cheerleaders.

The game's second quarter was notable for dogs, children, and goats running across the field. In the third quarter a dog seized the ball when it rolled out of bounds. Just the same, it was a famous victory, 6-2, for Navy. Rachel returned the goats to their owner and applied herself to more serious matters.

Her indebtedness to Chatham was growing. By the time she got her diploma, she would owe the school more than $1,600. Some of the remaining Carson land was held in Rachel's name. With her family's consent, she offered to sign over two of her Springdale lots to the college. This would be security for everything she owed now and would owe in June when she was graduated. Meanwhile she would try to find a buyer for the lots. If she did, she would pay off the whole debt in a lump. If she didn't, she would start making regular cash payments to the school beginning October 1, 1930, with 6 percent interest. The lots would be hers again when she wiped out the debt. Rachel and the school president, Cora Coolidge, signed a legal agreement to that effect on January 28, 1929. Both of them sighed with relief, for the same reason—Rachel's Bachelor of Arts degree was a certainty now.

Almost overnight, it seemed, the month was May. The weeks before commencement were full of good-news days. Rachel got word that Johns Hopkins University had granted her a year's scholarship as a graduate zoology student. When the *Arrow* editors put together their annual "Ideal College Senior," they borrowed "Rachel's brains" for their creation. At the end of May she was awarded her degree *magna cum laude*. There was a bonus, too. Chatham had arranged a summer-study fellowship for her at the Marine Biological Laboratory at Woods Hole on the extreme southwestern tip of Cape Cod. Woods Hole was then, as now, one of the world's most important centers for marine biological research. Along its waterfront at Great Harbor stood laboratories, libraries, and living quarters of the U.S. Bureau of Fisheries and the Marine Biological Laboratory, commonly referred to as MBL. Together they sheltered a scientific community that attracted the nation's most advanced investigators of the geology, geography, physics, chemistry, and biology of the oceans. Aboard the research vessels of both institutions scholars in dungarees dredged new knowledge from the depths of the Atlantic. Some of them were men whose names had become familiar to Rachel on the covers or in the pages of her textbooks.

The childhood sound of the seashell at her ear had never faded into silence. Now it had risen to a roar of promise guaranteed by the railroad timetable in her bureau drawer.

SEA LEVEL

Here we were born, here we were bred,
And the long dream started inside of our head.

—Virginia Moore

Maria Carson, turning the pages of the *Pennsylvanian,* paused to admire her daughter's graduation picture and the words printed alongside. She couldn't resist reading them aloud:

"A muse of fire that ascends
The brightest heavens of invention."

Rachel looked up from the small pile of books she was sorting. "That's over with. I'm descending to sea level." She spent June and two thirds of July in Springdale hemming dresses, doing chores for her family, reading books, making little farewell tours along her childhood trails on the Carson land.

It was still woodsy, though some of it had been cleared, with unpaved streets cut through. There seemed to be less wildlife, fewer birds, butterflies, squirrels. The grass, the fields, the trees in leaf seemed a little less green than she remembered.

There were dead trees in the apple orchard and many of the living ones looked discouraged. But most of the place still showed the pleasant marks of her father's hard outdoor work. The weeping mulberry tree in the front yard looked well. So did the rose-bushes her father had planted before she was born and had cultivated ever since. And she remembered the time he had won a citation for "the most beautiful lawn in the area" during some civic improvement campaign. There were no longer any pigs, cows, or horses in the Carson barnyard. Only a few chickens and a family of cats remained.

To Rachel, shopping along Pittsburgh Street, it seemed that Springdale had been a prettier place in her first-remembered childhood years. It did, in fact, look somewhat worse for the wear it had gotten in the three decades since the Carsons had settled there. But so did the rest of this once wildly beautiful valley of the lower Allegheny.

Three hundred years earlier, in the time of the first European arrivals, America's rivers were clean-looking liquid ribbons snaking their way through trackless mountains, woods, and fields. In their waters, in the air above them, behind the towering green-and-brown forest walls along their banks, there were riches of plant and animal life miraculously varied and numerous.

Now the Allegheny, for many miles upstream, was lined with industrial plants, towering smokestacks, mountainous piles of soft coal, huge storage tanks for chemicals, oil, and natural gas. Here and there sewage-disposal plants struggled to keep the land and the river not beautiful or pure but, please God, halfway sanitary. There were pumping-and-processing stations to make the water fit for human use by filtering and chemical treatment to kill dangerous bacteria.

The river itself looked dirty. The shore line between high and low water levels was a mucky compound of chemical waste from factory sewers, coal dust from storage yards, oily discharges from tugs, barges, tankers. Beyond the high watermark the tracks and fences of the railroad right-of-way cut off the towns from the river's edge. Everything between the river and the railroad was a sort of Dehumanized and Denaturized Zone that no one cared to enter except to earn his week's wages.

In places like New Kensington, Springdale, Acmetonia, Blawnox, and Harmarville, commercial buildings were strung along the main streets without plan, taste, or dignity. Their ugliness was softened only by grimy coatings of industrial fallout. Outdoors, on windless days, the sky looked like an unwashed window. But who ever stopped to wonder whether the haze hanging motionless overhead was man-made or nature's own?

Looking at her native valley with educated eyes, Rachel may have seen it for the first time not merely as a region of industrial progress but also as a place of biological blight. Well, people had to earn their living somehow. Robert and her father had worked at the West Penn Power Company's generating plant, whose smokestacks were Springdale's tallest structure. It was all too familiar, too long-established to worry about.

She was in no mood to mourn the beauties of southwestern Pennsylvania as the earliest explorers had seen them. Yet how grand, how overpoweringly, heart-wringingly beautiful this land must have been. Now it was just Springdale, sixteen sooty railroad miles from Pittsburgh, the city of steel mills and blast furnaces, whose skies were black by day and red at night. It was a little depressing but everybody agreed that this was the price of progress. Besides, Rachel thought, tomorrow she had to catch a train. It would take her over the mountains to see what she could see.

Her first destination was not Woods Hole but Baltimore. She registered at Johns Hopkins, introduced herself to Dr. R. P. Cowles of the zoology department, who was to be her academic adviser, then explored the campus and the city. She slept that night in Washington at the Skinker sisters' flat in the huge, dignified, old Ontario Apartments. She could not help seeing how different Washington was from Pittsburgh, even in that brief visit, but her mind raced eagerly beyond the capital city. Early the next morning she was on a bus that brought her to Luray, Virginia. Nearby Mary Skinker was vacationing at a mountain resort called Skyland, which could be reached only in a rattletrap carriage or on horseback. Rachel, calling on her pony-riding experience in the Krumpes' back yard, chose the latter. She wrote a long letter to Dorothy Thompson two weeks later in which she described the four-mile ride "up a rough forest road, where baby quail and even a wild turkey slipped off into the underbrush as I rode along . . . . I needn't tell you that the best part of the trip was when I saw Miss Skinker coming along the path to meet me!"

They spent their days riding horseback and playing tennis. "Playing with Miss Skinker has improved my game a little, anyway," Rachel reported. "She thinks she is no good, but she is." A hundred yards from their cabin there was a spot from which they could look straight down into the Shenandoah Valley. There were all sorts of thrilling peaks to which they could climb or ride "with glorious views from all of them." Most of all Rachel enjoyed sitting in front of the open fire and talking the evenings away with Miss Skinker. July's end was Skyland's end for both of them. They walked down the mountain and rode a bus together to Washington. After midnight Rachel boarded a train that brought her to New York City early in the morning.

Standing at the curb in front of Pennsylvania Station, looking uptown and down, she may well have wondered whether this island of Manhattan could support such immeasurable masses of brick, concrete, steel, and glass without sinking inch by inch into New York Bay. Ah well, it would certainly stay above water for her one-day visit to this man-made wonder of a city. After checking her baggage and breakfasting in the huge hotel across the street, she boarded a sightseeing bus that took her along Fifth

Avenue, Cathedral Parkway, Riverside Drive, and Broadway. She had lunch "at a funny German restaurant where the food was delicious but the menu was almost incomprehensible to me." Then she took the subway to Columbia University and climbed "the library steps I'd seen so often in pictures. Also the Cathedral of St. John the Divine, which I do not like. It's too *cold*."

Late afternoon found her in a stuffy little stateroom aboard the Colonial Line passenger boat bound for New Bedford. It was a cheaper, more interesting way than a train ride to reach Woods Hole. She remained on deck despite a pelting midsummer rain to see the Statue of Liberty as the boat steamed through New York Harbor toward the East River passage into Long Island Sound. The weather cleared after dark, and Rachel walked the deck for sheer solitary joy of being at sea, smelling salt air, and knowing she was beyond the sight of land. Then she went to bed.

At daybreak in New Bedford she was awake and ready to transfer to the Woods Hole boat. The sixteen-mile trip across Buzzards Bay in the clear, cold, early morning air was "glorious," though choppy water made walking across the deck an athletic feat.

The boat plowed a ruler-straight furrow across the bay to the Woods Hole passage, rounded Penzance Point, and entered the broad mouth of Great Harbor. It carried Rachel, wide-eyed at the sight, past the buildings of the U.S. Bureau of Fisheries and the

Marine Biological Laboratory, then moved with bulky self-confidence into Woods Hole Harbor. The rumble of engines backing water, the long, slow skree-eee-eeek of the boat rubbing against the dock pilings, and the rattle of winches told Rachel she had reached sea level at last, not merely as a spectator but as a participant.

Rachel went directly to the MBL office to register. That was Friday morning. By Sunday night she felt wonderfully at home. She liked everything—the town, the pleasant brick face of the main laboratory building, the library where "they seem to have everything"; the MBL dining hall, which provided three meals a day for seven dollars a week. A place to live was no problem. Mary Frye, her Chatham lab partner, was at Woods Hole on an undergraduate summer scholarship. They decided to share a rented room in the home of a middle-aged Cape Cod widow.

"One's mail is delivered to his laboratory table!" Rachel exulted in a letter to Dorothy Thompson. "So far I've only visited mine for the purposes of collecting mail, but tomorrow I begin. I expect to become very well acquainted with the turtle embryos that are waiting for me."

Her six weeks at MBL were joyously crowded with work, play, and planning for her first year at Johns Hopkins. She wrote to Dorothy Thompson again late in August.

"Mary and I are sitting on the beach adding to our sunburn. I've completely despaired of ever getting *brown*. However I am getting sort of weathered look-

ing, besides growing a crop of freckles . . . . Last
Sunday we had a beach party on one of the nearby
islands and it was great fun. Especially getting completely lost in the fog coming home." Their small
boat had almost been carried through the Woods
Hole passage into Buzzards Bay. "Mary and I played
tennis once, but I'm as rotten as ever. She is teaching
me to swim the crawl."

Most of the letter reported on more serious activities: "I've discovered that nothing has ever been done
on the terminal nerve of any reptile except the turtle,
so I've decided to work on it in lizards and snakes, and
maybe crocodiles. Meanwhile I'm working on a new
species of turtle and can use that for comparison."
She was also trying to complete her original project, a
study of the cranial nerves of the turtle that Dr.
Cowles thought would be worth publishing in a scientific journal.

"When I think of all the work that will have to be
done before I could publish anything . . . as a student of J.H.U. it makes me sort of sick . . . . It's no
cinch . . . . So much microscopic dissection is prov-
ing rather hard on my eyes." But, she added cheer-
fully, "It's all one grand experiment . . . I'm really
getting a little accomplished."

Busy or not she found time to study, alive, the creatures she had known at Chatham only as textbook
illustrations or as chemically preserved specimens. In
the aquarium of the U.S. Bureau of Fisheries, in the
MBL seawater specimen tanks, and on the beaches,
she could see them living their various, unbelievable

lives. She admired the graceful movements of the
fish, the continuous color-change of the squid, the
sliding motion of the starfish, the sea anemone's
flowerlike fringe of food-grabbing feelers.

She was delighted by the blue-eyed scallop's eyes,
as many as forty, running in two rows just behind the
wavy edges of its upper and lower shells. The underwater motion of these creatures was amusing. They
swam by opening their shells wide and clapping
them together smartly, squirting out little high-
pressure streams of water. Thus they went where
they would, jet-propelled, with a comical hopping
motion, gnashing their shells like fugitive sets of false
teeth declaring their independence on the run.

People from the U.S. Bureau of Fisheries lab also
took their meals at the MBL dining hall. It seemed to
Rachel that there was no other roof under which one
could find so many scientists who knew so much
about the ocean and its inhabitants. (She could not
help noticing, however, that there were few women
among them.) She knew that these were the people
she would like to work with after she got her Master's
degree.

The summer ended all too quickly. Rachel returned to Baltimore and found a place to live. Then
she went to Washington, D.C., to call on a man
named Elmer Higgins at the U.S. Bureau of Fisheries. As head of the bureau's Division of Scientific In-
quiry, he did not mind visits from students interested
in making biology their life's work.

To Higgins, as she entered his office, Rachel appeared gentle, almost timid, but mature in mind, speech, and manner.

"I have a Bachelor of Arts degree," she explained, "and will begin to work for my Master's degree in marine biology next month. I think I'd like to work in the fishery research field and I'd be grateful for any advice you can give me."

"What kind of advice, Miss Carson?"

Rachel asked a lot of questions. Why was fishery research worth doing? Why did the government support it? What kind of work was the fisheries bureau doing then? What future work was it planning? What opportunities were open to women as marine scientists in government or elsewhere? And could Mr. Higgins make any suggestions about choosing courses at Johns Hopkins that would help her qualify as a working marine biologist?

Higgins talked with her for an hour, outlining the scientific and technical problems of fishery research. He told her about his own years of work on the life histories of the shore fishes of the South Atlantic states. And he discussed the supporting basic sciences that a biologist specializing in his field ought to have.

One of Higgins' answers was what she had expected. Outside of high school and college teaching, or government work, there weren't many places for a lady biologist to go. She could pretty much forget about jobs in industry or even in museums. There was a decided feeling against women in the sciences, which were largely male-dominated. Even male biologists, who clearly understood the abilities of the females of other species, were unwilling to give up the ancient male prejudice against the female of *Homo sapiens.* Rachel found nothing discouraging in these facts. Marine biology was what she wanted, and that's what she was going to work at when she was ready.

Two weeks later Rachel began digging into her private mountain of academic work. Her classroom courses and scheduled laboratory periods— chemistry, comparative anatomy, botany, genetics —added up to a 46-hour week. In addition there were endless hours of outside reading and other class preparation. She rose at seven, ate breakfast at the university cafeteria, then went to her first class. Sometimes she hurried home at half past five to wash her face and change her clothes, sometimes not. Either way she spent most of her evenings in lab work, hoping to develop her study of the terminal nerve in one reptile or another to the point at which it would win Dr. Cowles' approval as a suitable pro- ject for her Master's thesis. She worked on lizard heads and on snakes, but neither she nor he was satis- fied with the results. She rejected his suggestion that she go to Florida, where she might work out her prob- lem by using loggerhead turtles. She had had enough of living in dormitories and furnished rooms and was busy persuading her family to move to Baltimore.

House hunting in the few weekend hours she could spare, she found "an out-of-town place" on the Old Philadelphia Road at Stemmer's Run. It was thirteen miles from Baltimore but only two miles from Chesapeake Bay. It had a grove of oak trees, a tennis court, and, indoors, a big open fireplace. It was somewhat isolated but there was dependable bus and train service for her daily trips to school. After a prolonged flurry of telegrams, special-delivery letters, and long-distance telephone conversations, Rachel overcame her parents' unreadiness to leave Springdale. Early in January 1930 the Carson family was reunited, except for brother Robert, whose business kept him in Pittsburgh.

A DIFFERENT BELL

We could smell the depression in the air . . . . It was like a raw wind; the very houses we lived in seemed to be shrinking, hopeless of any real comfort.

—HAROLD CLURMAN

The Johns Hopkins school bell ringing for Rachel early in October 1929 voiced a friendly challenge. Study! Learn! Get ready to do your chosen part in the world's work! But on Tuesday, October 29, all America heard the tolling of a different bell. The three o'clock closing gong of the New York Stock Exchange rang out disaster. In five hours of trading the prices of stocks that had climbed sky-high during Rachel's college years took the most sickening dive in Wall Street's 117-year history.

Factories and mines slowed down, then stopped entirely in the months that followed. As work stopped, wages stopped. More and more people were buying less and less. This brought other industries to a standstill. Because there was less spending power in the cities, farmers had to sell their products for less. Farmers, with shriveled incomes, bought fewer

factory-made goods, causing other cutbacks in industry and increasing the number of unemployed. Production and jobs, wages earned, and wages spent
spiraled dizzily downward until they hit bottom.
They stayed there during the years that became
known as The Great Depression.

Millions of families suddenly faced more oppres-
sive financial problems, with fewer solutions, than
they had ever experienced. In the Carson family
these problems revolved very closely around the
question of keeping Rachel in school, and some of the
solutions were of Rachel's making. By June 1930,
jobs of any kind were scarce everywhere. Nevertheless Rachel managed to find her first paying work as a
teaching assistant in the general biology course at the
Johns Hopkins Summer School.

> I've just put in a tough day at the lab [she wrote
> to Dorothy Thompson]. Getting the lab ready for
> 45 students is no fun. I have to do everything my-
> self. A lot of glassware needs washing, and I have to
> see to it that each table is supplied with a long list of
> apparatus. I have most of my lab material collected
> and I've learned a lot about the how and where of
> such things. I met Miss Lippy, my "boss" today, and
> she seems to be a very likeable sort of person, and I
> think will be very easy to work with.

Miss Lippy thought well of Rachel, too, and rehired
her for every summer school session through 1936.

Rachel started her second year at Johns Hopkins

with two urgent needs. One was a part-time job, which she found, as a lab assistant to Dr. Raymond Pearl, a geneticist. The other need was a workable research project for her Master's degree. Her experiments with turtle embryos, snakes, and lizards the year before had been nothing but a series of false starts. She had even attempted a study of the embryonic development of squirrels. It came to nothing because the squirrels sent to her by a Texas animal dealer would not breed. Without embryos there was nothing to research. She abandoned the project when she learned that her supplier could not send her any replacements because he had lost all his animals in a fire.

She explained to Dr. Cowles that she could not afford to waste any more time, and asked him to suggest another subject. Together they decided that she would produce a study of the pronephros of the channel catfish. Well, what was *that*? And why study it?

The *pronephros* is the fish's "temporary" kidney, which begins to develop two days after the egg has been fertilized. By the sixth day, the catfish outgrows its egg. With the help of its "temporary" kidney, which is now in good working order, it is able to live as a free-swimming larva. As this mere speck of a "mini-fish" keeps growing, a "permanent" kidney (the *mesonephros*) is also developing, closer to the tail end of the body cavity.

Little by little, the "permanent" kidney takes over the job of filtering the fish's body fluids to keep a proper balance of the chemicals it needs and to drain off useless or harmful chemicals. During this time the "temporary" kidney is slowly changing into something else. This "something else," in the adult fish, turns out to be the head kidney. It is so called because it lies toward the front of the body cavity, near the point where the skull joins the backbone. This is exactly the same space that has been occupied earlier by the pronephros.

In 1929 biologists were not at all sure of what the head kidney really was or what it did to earn its keep in the body of the adult fish. Did the "temporary" kidney itself gradually change into a head kidney? Or did the head kidney grow independently while the earlier one was just shriveling away? Did the head kidney continue to do some of the filtering work even though it was not put together like a kidney? Or did it become a blood-producing center?

Rachel did not hope to settle any of these points once and for all. She proposed merely to study the day-by-day growth of the pronephros from its beginning, in the egg, through its eleventh day, in the free-swimming larva. She would have to spend hundreds of hours examining thin slices of catfish egg and, later, of larva under a microscope. And she would have to read several thousand pages—in English, German, French, and Italian—about the physiology of the catfish. Her laboratory studies would enable her to write a complete and accurate description of how the "temporary" catfish kidney developed—up to the time that it began to disappear. Somebody else could take it from there, using older catfish to find out how the head kidney "moved in" to occupy the space being "vacated" by the pronephros. Such a future study, no doubt, would also turn up some reliable answers about what the head kidney really was.

Very early in 1931 Robert Carson rejoined the family group for a time. His business in Pittsburgh had become unprofitable, like tens of thousands of others throughout the land. He found a job in Baltimore as a radio-repairs estimator.

During those Depression-haunted days ordinary business transactions often took an unusual turn. One evening Robert came home carrying a handsome Persian cat, which he handed to Rachel. "Here's a present for you," he smiled. It was a welcome one. Rachel and her mother both were fond of cats. In Springdale there had always been one or more prowling their yard or arching its back in their kitchen.

Rachel couldn't resist asking where he got it. Robert explained he had accepted "Mitzi," a pedigreed female, as part payment on a twenty-dollar repair job. The deal was fifteen dollars in cash plus Mitzi.

Mitzi's earlier owner lived alone, worked all day, and didn't like to keep her pet shut in. And since it was she who suggested the trade she obviously liked radios better than cats. Mitzi and the kittens she bore later remained privileged members of the Carson household for many years.

There were less cheerful moments, however. In February 1931 Rachel was obliged to write to Chatham College that she could not send anything to reduce her debt to the college, even though she was working part time in Dr. Pearl's laboratory. "The difficulties which the wide-spread Depression and unemployment have brought to our household," she said, left her no choice. Her father was still trying to sell the two Springdale lots she had mortgaged to Chatham, and the family was trying to find other ways to begin making payment.

All through the academic year of fall 1930–spring 1931 Rachel worked at her paid job as lab assistant and at her own research. She studied hundreds of microscope slides that she had laboriously prepared and filled her notebooks with ideas and information. She also learned to make drawings with the help of a camera lucida—a camera without film, which carries the image of what it sees to a sheet of paper, permitting the user to trace the object with a pencil. It was slow, heavy going. She felt the strain and wished she could be a *full-time* graduate student. But in July she returned to her second summer as a Johns Hopkins teaching assistant. And when fall rolled around she needed another part-time job to help see her through her regular school year. Dr. Cowles came to the rescue with a pencil-written note to Professor C. J. Pierson at the University of Maryland in College Park:

> It is a pleasure for me to recommend to you Miss Rachel Carson who is applying for a position as half-time assistant in zoology at the University of Maryland. Miss Carson is a young lady of excellent char-

acter. She is pleasing in appearance and capable in everything that she does. Her scholarship has been high in her undergraduate studies and also in her graduate work here . . . . The students, both male and female, like and respect her, and Miss Grace Lippy, under whom she was assisting (in summer school), speaks very highly of her. I recommend Miss Carson to you without question.

She was hired in mid-September. Several times a week she made a seventy-mile round trip by bus or train from Stemmer's Run to College Park. She spent the rest of her long work week at Johns Hopkins, and at last, began to write her paper: "The Development of the Pronephros During the Embryonic and Early Larval Life of the Catfish (*Ictalurus punctatus*)." In the spring of 1932 it was finished—108 pages and 60 camera-lucida drawings, plus eight photomicrographs—photographs of very small objects, made with a camera fitted to a microscope.

Receiving her Master of Arts degree in marine zoology in June, Rachel was ready to do her chosen part of the world's work. But a part was not easily found in those Depression-ridden days. She would have to wait several years for the world to pull itself together.

In August she wrote to Chatham that she was still unable to make regular payments on her debt and that the school was free to sell her Springdale land whenever they saw fit, thus wiping out her obligation. Her half-time teaching job at the University of Maryland ended in December 1933. From then until late summer in 1935, her only employment as a scientist was at the Johns Hopkins summer school.

Millions of families lived in those years by "making a way out of no way"; by credit from the grocer and patience from the landlord; and by taking any kind of temporary, unsuitable, poorly paid jobs they could find. The Carsons were no worse off than some and much better off than many others. Through the fog of despair people were beginning to see a few glimmerings of hope that the country's prospects might start improving. It was only a question of time.

For the elder Robert Carson time ran out on the drizzly afternoon of July 6, 1935. Mrs. Carson, busy in the kitchen, looked up to see him walk uncertainly into the room.

"I feel ill. I need some air." He walked, gasping for breath, toward the back door. His wife followed him watchfully, at a distance. He crossed the small backyard patio, then pitched face forward into the grass. She ran to his side, helped him roll over, and cradled him in her arms. They were alone. Did she dare leave him to telephone or to run down the road crying out for help? She didn't need to decide. He died moments later, while she held him, in the gentle summer rain.

A telephone message brought Rachel hurrying home from her laboratory job at Johns Hopkins. At dusk she walked through the grassy back yard. Here, near the fence, was where he had helped her dig earthworms by flashlight for her biology students

Mrs. Carson with Marian, Rachel, and Robert, about 1910

Rachel, aged five, with her dog Candy

At seven, in a Sunday dress her mother made

The Little Brown House.

Once upon a time, two little wrens were hunting a little house to set up housekeeping. All at once they saw a dear little brown house with a green roof. "Now that is just what we need," said Mr. Wren to Jenny.

Rachel wrote "The Little Brown House" when she was in the second grade

This drawing of a red catchfly was made when Rachel was nine

"FIRESIDE DREAMS"
BY
R.L.CARSON.

A pensive self-portrait, drawn when Rachel was ten

Rachel at fifteen, with a favorite teacher, Marguerite Howe of the Springdale High School

Playing with her dog Rags, Maryland, 1945

In Falmouth, Massachusetts, soon after the publication of
The Sea Around Us. © *1951 Edwin Gray*

With Dorothy Freeman (left) and Roger, off Boothbay, Maine, summer 1958

Feeding the gulls on her beach at West Southport, Maine

Rachel Carson on her "wildwood lot" in West Southport

to dissect. Here was . . . and there were . . . so many times and places . . . small happenings . . . father . . . father . . . Grief is long on remembrance and short on words.

SONG OF THE SEA

*This writing is an unnatural business.
It makes your head hot and your feet
cold, and it stops the digesting of your
food.*

—JOHN BURROUGHS

Elmer Higgins remembered Rachel when she walked into his office. "You're the young lady who came to see me a few years ago when you were just starting your graduate work—at Johns Hopkins I believe it was. Marine zoology, right?"

"Quite right, Mr. Higgins. It's kind of you to remember."

"Well! Sit down. What can I do for you this time?"

"I have my Master's degree. I've been teaching general biology at Johns Hopkins and zoology at the University of Maryland. But my situation has changed recently. My father died in July, and half-time university employment isn't enough to take care of my mother and me."

Higgins was a man of lively sympathies. The tilt of his head invited her to go on.

"Do you have a position for which I might qualify?

Having asked your advice about what to study, and having taken it, it seems logical for me to come back to you now."

He was impressed by the directness of her attack. She deserved "man-to-man" treatment.

"Can you write?" he asked.

"I also majored in English at college."

"Were you any good?"

"I got A's in all my English courses."

Higgins kept a straight face but he smiled inwardly.

Quite a girl, he thought: ladylike appearance, modest manner, soft voice. She must be very sure of herself to offer such brief, unflustered answers to his challenging questions.

"Fine," he said. "We'll *see* if you can write. Let me explain."

In an unguarded moment Commissioner Frank T. Bell had instructed the Bureau of Fisheries to prepare fifty-two radio broadcasts about fishery and marine life. Higgins became responsible for the planning and writing of the series. He and his staff called them "Seven-Minute Fish Tales," though they were presented on the air as "Romance Under the Waters." Knowing nothing about marine biology, the professional radio writer hired by Higgins soon ran out of ideas. The staff scientists knew nothing about writing for nonscientific radio listeners. Higgins managed somehow to meet his weekly deadline for mailing new scripts to the radio stations, though many of them made pretty dreary listening. It struck him that this girl might just be able to bridge the gap between good science and good writing.

Higgins discussed the kind of stories and the style of writing he wanted. Then he outlined Rachel's first three assignments. "What I'm offering you is part-time, temporary employment at the rate of $1,000 a year," he explained. (Rachel made a mental note that this came to $19.25 a week.) Higgins went on: "You can work at home if you prefer or in our department library. Come back at the beginning of the week. If I can use what you've written there'll be quite a number of others for you to do."

Rachel rode back to Stemmer's Run feeling lighter-hearted than she had for months. Total unemployment was no longer whispering threats into her ear.

Reading Rachel's efforts the following week, Elmer Higgins kept muttering "fine, fine" as he turned page after page. Finally, looking up: "I think these'll do very nicely, Miss Carson. Here's your next assignment."

What would happen to her $19.25-a-week job when the series was finished, Rachel wondered? Time would tell. Meanwhile the bureau decided that the radio scripts could be turned into a substantial brochure to be issued through the Government Printing Office. Higgins asked Rachel to rewrite and edit the broadcast material to give it a really attractive literary style. While she was at this chore, a civil service examination was announced for the job of junior aquatic biologist, grade P-1 in departmental lingo. (The Bureau of Fisheries was then a subdivision of the Department of Commerce. In 1939 it was transferred to the Department of the Interior. A year later it was merged with the Bureau of Biological Survey to form the Fish and Wildlife Service.)

Rachel, the only woman taking the exam, was the highest-scoring candidate. Higgins requested that she be assigned to his office. She was appointed as a full-time permanent civil service employee at $2,000 a year on August 17, 1936. She noted cheerfully that for the next eighteen months she would be earning $38.48 a week—every week. After that she would be eligible for a small length-of-service raise. And if the department had any merit-increase money to spread around, she was sure she would manage to get her share. She and her mother continued to need it.

When Rachel finished editing the "fish tales" pamphlet, Higgins asked her to write an introduction that would tie all the stories together like beads on a string. Well, that seemed simple enough. The stories were about sea creatures. The sea makes their existence possible. The sea's watered-down chemicals nourish animal and vegetable lives of pinpoint size; the sea feeds them to larger animals, who become food for still larger or more clever animals. And it is the sea from which birds and the cleverest of all animals, men, can seize vast amounts and varieties of food for their almost countless populations.

Rachel, very pleased with what she had written, sat in Higgins' office waiting for him to finish reading it. At last he looked up at her solemnly.

"Miss Carson, it's not suitable."

Rachel could not mask her disappointment.

"I thought it was pretty good," she gulped.

Higgins, still solemn, replied, "That's the trouble. It's more than pretty good. This is such a beautiful piece of writing, so poetic, colorful, and graphic in its descriptions of the sea that it makes the stories you are introducing seem very dull by comparison."

Rachel was silent but the sudden sagging of her shoulders said, "I don't believe you!" Then, as she met Higgins' earnest face, she smiled with thousand-watt brightness.

"I think what you've written is a piece of literature," Higgins said. "I propose that you keep it as your own property, but since you wrote it on government time, I want you to write a simpler introduction for the fish tales on your own time."

She answered with a hint of still-unbelieving laughter in her voice. "Of course, I'll be glad to. But what will I do with this piece of literature, as you call it?"

"Send it to a magazine. Somebody will pay money for it."

"Oh, my, do you really think so? Which magazine?"

"I'm sure someone will want it. Why not start at the top? Send it to *The Atlantic Monthly*."

Higgins was paying her a dazzling compliment. The *Atlantic* was America's most distinguished literary magazine. It had maintained its reputation since its earliest appearance a few years before the Civil War. Its list of contributors was a virtual *Who's Who* of American literature that in earlier times had in-

cluded such names as Ralph Waldo Emerson, Henry
David Thoreau, John Greenleaf Whittier, and
James Russell Lowell.

Rachel kept her composure. "Thanks, Mr. Higgins. Thank you very much. I guess I'd better get
back to my mail queries."

Questions about fish, fishery, fish cookery, fish culture, the care of pet goldfish; questions about the
mating, breeding, feeding, and fighting habits of
every conceivable freshwater, tidewater, and deepsea creature imaginable flowed through the U.S.
mails in a steady stream to Elmer Higgins' division.
Thousands of these letters could be answered by
sending leaflets and booklets that were already in
print. It was Rachel's job to deal with more complicated inquiries, which called for library research.
When Higgins' staff noticed a large number of letters
asking pretty much the same questions, the bureau
ordered the preparation of a new piece of printed
matter to cover the subject.

At home that evening, Rachel read her rejected introduction again and thought well, yes, it's good—
but good enough for the *Atlantic*? Not likely. She put
the manuscript away and turned to more urgent
business.

During the Depression years Rachel had made no
effort to write anything for sale. Publishers weren't
buying manuscripts, especially from beginners, because people weren't buying books or magazines if
they could avoid it. The printed word had become

something of an extravagance in this period when bread was not easily obtained. Even established writers and some rather famous ones were glad to take jobs on the Federal Arts projects set up to help unemployed writers and editors. But Higgins' question—"Can you write?"—uncorked her long-bottled urge to put deeply felt, carefully chosen, artfully arranged words on paper.

One way or another, much of the material published through the Government Printing Office had to do with biology, simply because all human life depends directly or indirectly on the other living things of land and water. Usually these publications were meant for readers with little or no scientific knowledge. Unfortunately, they were often written by scientific workers with little or no literary talent. This was certainly true of many fisheries-bureau pamphlets Rachel had to read in her first months as a "temporary."

Slowly she realized that Higgins had given her a job not because she was a biologist nor because she was a writer, but because she was both. At the same time he had given her a clue to harmonious living with her twin loves, art and science. She knew now, beyond any doubt, that she had something everlastingly worthwhile to write about—something as rich in real-life beauty as anything that poets could imagine.

Meanwhile, early in 1936, she began to sell writings of a more modest kind to the Sunday magazine section of *The Baltimore Sun*. The first of these, which carried Rachel's by-line, was headlined, "It'll Be Shad-Time Soon—and Chesapeake Bay Fishermen Hope for Better Luck This Season." It wove American history, the life-cycle of the shad, and a knowing description of commercial-fishing techniques into a very readable story. The poor luck of shad fishermen in preceding years, she wrote, "is probably the result of destructive methods of fishing, the pollution of waters by industrial and civic wastes, and the development of streams for water power and navigation."

Mark Watson, the Sunday editor, bought other articles when he could, which was not very often. In the second half of the year he bought nothing. It is doubtful that Rachel was ever paid more than twenty-five dollars for an article. Ten or fifteen was the more usual rate. But it was ready money and she needed it.

The distance between Stemmer's Run and Washington was too great for a working girl to travel twice a day. Rachel and her mother took an attractive two-story house at the corner of Highland Avenue and the Colesville Road in Silver Spring, Maryland. The rent was higher but there were two added permanent members of the household, Marian Virginia Williams and Marjorie Louise Williams. They were the grammar-school-age daughters of Rachel's older sister, Marian. Gay, laughing Marian had married while Rachel was still at college. She had died of a chronic illness at the untimely age of forty. Rachel and her mother thought it would be good for the girls to live with them.

One lean day in 1937 Rachel remembered her little "fish tales" essay, made a few minor changes suggested by Higgins, titled it "Undersea," and mailed it to *The Atlantic Monthly.* Six weeks later she received a check for seventy-five dollars and a note telling her the piece would appear in the magazine's September issue. Higgins was delighted.

"Well, you're going to write a book now, aren't you?"

"I've always wanted to but . . . "

"You've got one started, Miss Carson. Take this little essay, divide it into the subjects you've only touched on, and write a full chapter about each. There's your book right there! This article is really the outline for a complete story of marine ecology."

Ecology is the study of living things in relation to their environment and to each other. Man, always a land animal, could not help learning a good deal about the land environment in which he farmed and hunted for food. Yet, though he also took vast amounts of food and other necessities from the sea, he knew relatively little about the bewildering web of oceanic life and how the sea supported it. After thousands of years the miracle of the loaves was quite familiar. The miracle of the fishes still needed to be more deeply understood, more widely appreciated. To this end, Higgins felt, Rachel's essay could be a real contribution.

Higgins was not alone. Hendrik Willem van Loon, one of the most successful writers and brilliant personalities of his day, had also read "Undersea." He was impressed by sentences such as this: "Already the terns were milling about overhead in a noisy cloud, like hundreds of scraps of paper flung to the wind." As author of *The Story of Mankind,* then in its forty-ninth printing, Van Loon's judgment counted for something in the offices of his publisher, Simon & Schuster. Van Loon felt that R. L. Carson, whoever *that* was, had an unusual talent for writing about nature. He said as much to editor-in-chief Quincy Howe.

Howe wrote to Rachel. Rachel wrote to both men. Van Loon wrote to her. A brisk three-way flow of correspondence developed. In a subsequent letter Rachel outlined, very briefly, her idea for a book telling the story of the lives that are lived on the shores and surfaces of the sea, in its depths, and in the air above.

In mid-January Rachel asked Higgins for a day off and traveled to Old Greenwich, Connecticut, for a more detailed discussion of her project with Van Loon and Quincy Howe. She stayed overnight, then hurried back to Washington, delighted with Mrs. Van Loon's hospitality and with the warm approval both men had given to her general plan. She was still a long way, however, from getting an author's contract that guaranteed publication of the book. Before that happened she would have to develop her plan in greater detail and write one or more chapters.

She worked at it weekends and evenings after her tiring eight-hour day in the Bureau of Fisheries. There were months of painstaking research to assemble the known and probable facts. That was the science part of it. The facts had to be arranged in a scientifically correct but lifelike pattern. That was half art, half science. But only the actual labor of her writing could make her readers feel what she felt about the endless drama of life and death in the ocean; about the poetry of the fishes' struggle, or the birds', to grow from egg to adult. If she *wrote* successfully—that would be all art.

In February 1938 she asked Van Loon if he could help her get an advance payment from the publisher. If so, she could give all her free time to working on her book instead of using some of it to write "the newspaper things" on which she was relying for extra income. The advance would also give her money for a trip south. In June, while the publisher was still thinking about her request, she traveled to the U.S. Bureau of Fisheries station at Beaufort, North Carolina, to collect more firsthand material.

At least seven times that year, however, she had to put aside her book project to write Sunday articles for *The Baltimore Sun.* They bore such headlines as "Ducks Are on the Increase but the Short Hunting Season Will Continue"; "Chesapeake Eels Seek the Sargasso Sea"; "Walrus and Carpenter Not Oysters' Only Foe"; "Whalers Ready for Season."

It was quite a while before Simon & Schuster sent her $250 (after seeing one chapter and a full outline of the rest of the book). They would not sign a contract to publish it, however, until they had seen several more chapters.

Rachel was finding out the hard way whether she really wanted to be a writer or not. Nights and weekends, she kept at it, managing betweentimes to do more articles for the *Sun*. Early in 1940 she had finished five chapters, about twenty-two thousand words. Maria Carson, now seventy-one, but lively as ever, typed the manuscript and sent it off. Quincy Howe, who had never been less than enthusiastic, was more so than ever, and Max L. Schuster gave his final approval. At last it happened. A contract came in the mail. Rachel signed and returned it, and a check for $250 followed.

The writing went much faster now. She had a deadline to meet. Through the last half of 1940 she also corresponded with artists about illustrations for the book. She persuaded the publisher to accept Howard Frech, a staff artist on the *Sun,* but she took no chances. She sent him lists of reference books in which to check the scientific accuracy of his finished drawings. They were every bit as good as she had dared hope. Meanwhile her mother typed the remaining chapters.

The finished manuscript of Rachel's first book, *Under the Sea Wind,* was in the publisher's hands early in 1941. There was nothing to do now but wait until the mail carrier delivered the customary number of free author's copies. When they arrived, Rachel handed one of them to her mother. Holding it, Maria Carson could hardly help thinking of the time twenty-three years earlier when *St. Nicholas* had published her daughter's juvenile writing efforts.

Mrs. Carson glanced at the first few pages of the book. Then she looked at her daughter and smiled, "Thank you, Rachel." *Under the Sea Wind* was dedicated: "To My Mother."

Rachel entered her chief's office at the fisheries bureau the next morning and handed him a copy of the book. It was inscribed: "To Mr. Higgins, who started it all. Rachel L. Carson. November 6, 1941."

The world's library shelves were not lacking in fine books about the sea written by navigators, historians, scientists, poets, novelists. But with rare exceptions they were written from the human point of view.

Under the Sea Wind was different. Rachel had succeeded in thinking her way aloft and underwater to picture the ocean world from the point of view of its inhabitants. She wrote as though she were a correspondent who had lived with a flock of frail shore birds on their exhausting 8,000-mile migration from Patagonia to the Arctic Circle:

> While the tide was still ebbing, the sanderlings fed on the island beach . . . . As they slept, and as the earth rolled from darkness to light, birds from many feeding places were hurrying along the flyways . . . . All through the night the cries of curlews and plovers and knots, of sandpipers and turnstones and yellowlegs, drifted down from the sky . . . . About an hour before dawn the sanderling flock gathered together on the island beach . . . . The little band of brown-mottled birds mounted into the darkness and, as the island grew small beneath them, set out toward the north.

Rachel did not linger below. She was their flight companion and they remained life-sized in her view.

She recorded the terrors of an early spring snow-storm in the arctic nesting grounds. Two sanderlings, Silverbar the female and Blackfoot the male, are among the survivors, but tragedy visits the nest of two snowy owls, hunters of other birds and small animals:

The snow death had taken many lives . . . . The hen had been brooding six eggs for more than a week. During the first night of wild storm the snow had drifted deep about her . . . the owl remained on her nest, warming the eggs with her great body . . . . Now Ookpik, the cock owl, called to his mate with low, throaty cries . . . . It took many minutes to free herself from the snow and to climb, half fluttering, half stumbling out of the nest . . . .

As the snow fell on the still-warm eggs and the hard bitter cold gripped them, the life fires of the tiny embryos burned low. The crimson streams ran slower in the vessels that carried the racing blood from the food yolks to the embryos. After a time there slackened and finally ceased the furious activity of cells that grew and divided to make owl bone and muscle and sinew. The pulsating red sacs under the great oversized heads hesitated, beat spasmodically, and were stilled. The six little owls-to-be were dead in the snow, and by their death, perhaps, hundreds of unborn lemmings, ptarmigans, and arctic hares had the greater chance of escaping death from the feathered ones that strike from the sky.

How did life underwater look, feel, taste, and sound to Scomber, the baby mackerel, growing large enough in coastal waters to make his way to the open sea?

> As yet Scomber knew little of the world in which he lived . . . of the difference between night and day or the sea's surface and its depths . . . . On the tenth morning of his life he had lingered in the upper fathoms . . . . Out of the clear green water a dozen gleaming silver fishes suddenly loomed up. They were anchovies, small and herring-like. The foremost anchovy caught sight of Scomber . . . . In a fraction of a second he would have been seized and eaten but a second anchovy . . . collided with the first and in the confusion Scomber dashed beneath them . . . . ''

Darting downward, the little mackerel escapes from a few anchovies to find himself in the midst of thousands. These have no urge to eat him at the moment because they are desperately busy trying to keep themselves from being eaten:

> A pack of young bluefish had picked up the scent . . . . The leader of the bluefish lunged. With a snap of razor-toothed jaws he seized two of the anchovies. Two clean-severed heads and two tails floated away. The taste of blood was in the water . . . a strange new taste . . . drawn in by Scomber with the water he passed through mouth and gills . . . disquieting to a small fish that had

never tasted blood or experienced the lust of the hunter.

Man appeared briefly in Rachel Carson's pages, and only as a super beast of prey. Yet one man, a mackerel fisherman, had the quality of wonder in him that distinguishes his kind of creature from all others on earth:

He sometimes thought about the fish as he looked at them on deck or being iced down in the hold. What had the eyes of the mackerel seen? Things he'd never see; places he'd never go . . . . It seemed to him incongruous that a creature that had made a go of life in the sea, that had run the gauntlet of all the relentless enemies . . . should at last come to death on the deck of a mackerel seiner, slimy with fish gurry and slippery with scales. But after all, he was a fisherman . . . .

Chapter after chapter, Rachel led her readers to experience the ocean's cycles of light and darkness, of tides and seasons, of warmth and cold; and to understand them as forces that keep in motion the endless drama of birth, growth, self-preservation, death—and new birth under the sea wind.

The reviews were favorable, though some chose to split a few hairs. In the *Saturday Review of Literature* William Beebe, marine biologist and underseas explorer, wrote: "I have thoroughly enjoyed every word of the volume but I found difficulty in reading it out loud." He did add, "Miss Carson's science cannot be questioned."

Despite this minor criticism, Dr. Beebe included two of her chapters three years later in his *Book of Naturalists,* a collection of the world's finest writing about nature. Rachel found it amusing that Beebe's book "began with Aristotle and ended with Carson." In the years that followed, Rachel and Beebe kept up a warm personal and professional correspondence.

The New York Times said of *Under the Sea Wind:* "It promises its readers knowledge and sound enjoyment." Rachel also had good reason to be pleased with the New York *Herald Tribune* review: "There is drama in every sentence. She rouses our interest in this ocean world and we want to watch it."

Her moment of triumph, however, was abruptly ended by more urgent public events. Japanese planes sank the American fleet at Pearl Harbor on December 7. Overnight the nation found itself at war. Nazi submarines were prowling the Atlantic close to American shores. The oceans had become a place not of fearsome natural grandeur but of man-made terror.

Rachel's intricate and lovely sea-wind song could not make itself heard above the thunder of navy guns and the roar of bombing planes. Five thousand copies were sold. Then the book was quickly forgotten by her publisher, the critics, and the reading public.

FISH AND WILDLIFE
IN WASHINGTON

*Most men, it seems to me, do not care
for nature and would sell their share in
all her beauty for a given sum. Thank
God men have not yet learned to fly so
they can lay waste the sky as well as the
earth.*

—Henry David Thoreau

In her first three years of government service Rachel
was promoted three steps. A 1939 memorandum by
Charles E. Jackson, acting commissioner of the fisheries bureau, said: "She has keen analytical abilities
and unusual skill in the interpretation of scientific
results. The character and quality of her work in the
field of general fishery biology and her usefulness to
the bureau have increased rapidly . . . . "

Rachel became doubly valuable as thousands of
male government employees were suddenly transferred to special wartime jobs after Pearl Harbor. On
Higgins' recommendation, though he hated to lose
her, she was upgraded again in May 1942, becoming

an assistant to the chief of the Office of Information in the Fish and Wildlife Service. In August the service and many of its staff were transferred to Chicago to make room in Washington for wartime government agencies. For two years Rachel and her mother lived in Evanston, a Chicago suburb.

Wars are fought with food as well as weapons. Hundreds of thousands of tons of meat were going overseas to support American, British, and Soviet troops, creating shortages at home. Strange substitutes began to appear in American markets—whale, buffalo, reindeer, moose, to be used for steaks, stews, soups, fricassees. These outlandish goodies were even scarcer and less attractive than the unappetizing choices of familiar meat available at neighborhood butcher shops. As a matter of wartime government policy it became necessary to make fish more popular in stateside civilian menus.

It was Rachel's assignment to provide ammunition for this campaign. Between 1943 and 1945 she wrote four pamphlets totaling two hundred pages in which she described sixty-five fresh- and salt-water fishes and a dozen kinds of shellfish. Together they were a four-part *Who's Who* of American fishes. The pamphlets had chapters on the nutritional value of fish and expert advice on how to buy, prepare, and serve it. But the greater part of each guide was devoted to the life stories of the fishes themselves. In Rachel's introduction to the first of the series she wrote: "Before we can try new foods, we must know what they are. Our enjoyment of these foods is heightened if we also know something of the creatures from which they are derived, how and where they live, how they are caught, their habits and migrations."

Rachel's fish booklets were very successful. They were used by newspaper and magazine editors and by radio broadcasters to help change the food prejudices of America's meat-eating millions.

She could not convince herself, however. In later years, after she had become famous for her writings about the sea, she confessed that she would be delighted if her hosts didn't serve seafood when she came to dinner. She had never cared for it much.

People engaged in killing each other in almost countless numbers cannot help destroying some part of nature, too, since nature itself provides the war materials and the battlegrounds. More terribly than it had ever done in peacetime, the United States at war overused, misused, polluted, and neglected its plains, forests, rivers, and seacoasts with no thought of the future. The war ended but the damage went on. It became urgent that the government should talk about conserving the nation's resources and about changing America's carefree attitude toward its natural environment.

Hunters and fishermen were becoming more plentiful than deer in the woods or perch in the lakes. Worse, farmlands were being bulldozed, mountaintops leveled, woodlands gouged, marshlands filled, and swamps drained to build vast new Levittowns, tract developments, industrial parks. Millions of people were leaving overcrowded, run-down cities to live in these new instant suburbs or in old ones. Millions of automobiles were pouring off the assembly lines to carry the new suburbanites to and from their city jobs. Rivers of concrete were being poured to form turnpikes, highways, throughways, freeways, causeways, and bridges.

The small animals who held out in their shrinking homegrounds found dangerous neighbors among these newly arrived city folk. For squirrels who raided bird-feeders, for raccoons and possums who overturned garbage cans, the penalty could be death by poison or by mail-order rifle.

The wholesale slaughter of birds and beasts for profit, crop protection, or coldhearted fun is as old as the white man's first footprint on this continent, and as new as next fall's hunting season. The eastern buffalo was wiped out by 1800. The western buffalo population, 60 million in colonial times, was down to a pitiful herd of 20 before it was saved by federal law. (There are now 12,000 or more.) The last passenger pigeon, whose numbers once were estimated at 5 billion, died in a zoo in 1914. No human eye has beheld a Carolina parakeet since 1920, though there were once hundreds of thousands. The death of a mateless male heath-hen in 1932 put an eternal end to its kind, once numerous in New York and New England, but too edible for its own good. The golden grizzly bear is gone from California and the Merriam elk from Arizona. Dozens of other species and varieties in fur or feathers have also vanished. Dozens more continue to be threatened with extinction. The list changes from year to year.

As far back as the 1880's the federal government took steps to protect places in which the natural plant-and-animal communities were still unharmed by human invasion. For fifty years the kind of lawmaking, scientific research, and land management needed to conserve wildlife moved ahead, though the pace was slow and faltering. During World War II this effort came to a standstill.

Now, however, the Fish and Wildlife Service turned from encouraging housewives to serve more fish to the touchier task of educating their husbands on the subject of wildlife conservation. Rachel planned a series of twelve booklets under the general title of *Conservation in Action*. Several were devoted to one or another of the expanding network of national bird and animal refuges, of which there are hundreds today. Rachel found time to write four or five of them herself after her return from Chicago to Washington, in the years between 1947 and 1950.

Her brief introductory note to the series was a gentle plea for peaceful coexistence with nature: "Wild creatures, like men, must have a place to live. As civilization creates cities, builds highways, and drains marshes it takes away, little by little, the land that is suitable for wildlife. And as their spaces for living dwindle, the wildlife populations themselves decline."

Her simple reminder of the need for human decency toward other forms of life was a statement that the Fish and Wildlife Service cherished and continued to use in its publications for a quarter of a century.

Rachel's sympathy toward all living things found other, more direct expressions. Her colleagues realized how deeply personal these feelings were the morning she came to work with fresh bloodstains on her clothing. Driving from her home in Silver Spring to her office in the Department of the Interior building, she saw a dog struck by an auto. While dozens of other motorists sped by, she stopped, carried the injured animal into her car, and drove to a veterinary hospital. Unable to find the owner at the time, she paid for the dog's medical care herself. She was not a one-woman Humane Society. She was simply a humane woman who believed in Henry Thoreau's advice: "Rescue the drowning and tie your shoestrings."

Rachel Carson also kept the shoestrings of her government job well tied, a fact that the Fish and Wildlife Service recognized once again by making her editor-in-chief of its Information Division.

When Bob Hines, a talented wildlife artist, was about to join the service in July 1948, Frank Dufresne, director of the Information Division, warned him, "You're going to have a lady supervisor."

"In that case," said Hines, "let's forget the whole thing."

"You'll be making a great mistake if you let that stop you," Dufresne replied. "You'd better come with us anyway."

Hines was at his drawing board for two weeks before he met his new boss. Returning from a research trip to the Pacific coast, Rachel walked into his office, put out her hand, and introduced herself. "I'm Rachel Carson. Welcome to Washington."

"It was just that abrupt and clean," Hines remembered. "My impression was immediately favorable, but naturally I reserved judgment about her as my supervisor." It was the beginning of a deeply satisfying professional and personal association for both of them.

"She was a very able executive with almost a man's administrative qualities," Hines decided after a time. "She knew how to get things done the quickest, simplest, most direct way. She had the sweetest, quietest 'no' any of us had ever heard. But it was like Gibraltar. You didn't move it. She had no patience with dishonesty or shirking in any form and she didn't appreciate anybody being dumb. But she always showed much more tolerance for a dull-minded person who was honest than for a bright one who wasn't. She didn't like shoddy work or shoddy behavior. She was just so doggone good she couldn't see why other people couldn't try to be the same. She had *standards*, high ones."

This was the office image of Rachel Carson, for whom her staff of six, Hines among them, developed an intense loyalty that she returned in kind.

As editor-in-chief she was responsible for good writing, accurate information, and attractive printed appearance in all material published by the Fish and Wildlife Service. That meant everything, from one-page leaflets offering fish-cookery hints to large scientific studies of various forms of marine life. Even in the case of scientific reports she was free to question the writing style or the quality of the scientific information if she had a good reason. Her own scientific knowledge and her technical abilities as an editor were important in this respect.

She did not hesitate to reprimand at least one widely respected fish biologist for sending her a manuscript that violated Government Printing Office regulations as to typing, use of abbreviations, and preparation of drawings. The fact that he out-ranked her in the world of science troubled her not at all.

Once, riffling through a batch of just-finished work Hines had brought her, she held up his drawing of a mullet and said, "We'd better fix this one, Bob. You've put one spine too many in the dorsal fin." She was right.

She worked in a spacious oblong office of the Interior building, at a large table in the light of tall windows behind her. Generous stretches of book-shelves followed the lines of the two long walls. Close to her main entrance door these walls were inter-rupted by inside doors for easy communication with Hines on one side, and with her secretary on the other. Neither door was often closed. The room itself was bare of decoration except for a large framed photograph of a blue crab.

Rachel ran an orderly office but never a fussy one. The piles of manuscript, correspondence, and mis-cellaneous paperwork on her desk were less than checkerboard-neat, yet she never had to scurry around trying to find things. She knew where they were.

Leaving her office for any reason at all, she fol-

lowed a little ritual that seemed appealingly femi-
nine to those who noticed. On her way out she opened
a narrow door concealing a washstand mirror. She
checked her hair and her discreetly applied makeup,
lingering for a few quick sweeps of her hairbrush or a
dab of lipstick if necessary. Then she was on her way,
her footfalls making "a very distinctive sound." Hines
could always tell when it was Rachel coming down
the corridor.

"She had a very forceful walk. It wasn't any of that
high-heel clippety-clop but it was direct. No hesita-
tion. She moved straight to where she was going. I
think that was just the pattern of her life."

THE SEA AROUND HER

For the sea too seeks and rejoices,
Gains and loses and gains,
And the joy of her heart's own choice is
As ours, and as ours are her pains:
As the thoughts of our hearts are her
  voices,
And as hers is the pulse of our veins.

—ALGERNON CHARLES SWINBURNE

Under the Sea Wind had been a disappointment.
Rachel did not doubt the merit of that first effort but
its short sales-life and her publisher's lack of interest
kept her from trying again. The more so since her
government job as a writer-editor-executive gave her
solid satisfactions. Best of all, it made knowledge and
news of the ocean a daily, continuing part of her life.

For twenty years Rachel had made the most of her
opportunities to study the sea, not only in print but
directly, with her own senses. She spent summer
weeks in the laboratories and aboard the scientific research boats at Woods Hole. On government business
she visited eastern fisheries stations, aquatic wildlife
refuges, and the California coast of the Pacific. Alone,
she wandered unmeasured miles of Atlantic beaches.

The more she learned, the more fascinated she became with what was known and what was not known about the sea. The feeling built up until she could no longer contain it. It demanded expression of a kind for which there was little opportunity in her official writing. After all, why would the United States government want to publish the story of her since-childhood love affair with the sea and its life?

Win or lose, she could no longer keep from writing another book about the sea. She wanted it to be "a book for anyone who has looked out upon the ocean with wonder, from the deck of a liner or a troop transport, or has stood on the shore alone with the waves and his thoughts, or has felt from afar the fascination of the sea . . . a book that I myself searched for on library shelves but never found . . . that will be easily understood and imaginatively appealing to the reader untrained in science."

She started work in the summer of 1948. The beauty and the accuracy of the sentences she put on paper did not come easily. She was a slow, self-critical writer who worked best in the hours when the rest of the world was not awake to interrupt her. Sometimes she went sleepless from her desk at home to her office in the Interior building. Nevertheless, the sheets of manuscript rolling from her typewriter began to make a promising little pile. By the end of the year she had enough to show to a publisher.

She decided to find a literary agent, a professional who looks after the interests of writers in their dealings with publishers. Mrs. Marie Rodell, in New

York, newly established as an agent but thoroughly experienced in the publishing world, agreed to represent her. She brought the far-from-finished manuscript, after rejection by two or three other publishers, to Philip Vaudrin, an executive editor at Oxford University Press. He was enthusiastic, though some of his associates saw small chance of commercial success for Rachel's project. Nevertheless, Vaudrin offered her a contract after sending her sample chapters to Daniel Merriman, director of the Bingham Oceanographic Laboratory at Yale University, and asking for his opinion. Mr. Merriman replied:

> Miss Carson writes attractively and has the knack of explaining complex matters with great ease . . . . I should say there is a clear place for this book. It seems to give every promise of being a far better piece of work [for nonscientist readers] than any other on the subject in recent times.

The "complex matters" were those of a relatively new field of learning—oceanography—which is nothing less than the total study of the sea, from its guessable beginnings to the present:

> Its size, shape, surfaces, and depths.
> Its currents, waves, and tides.
> Its underwater mountain ranges, valleys, and volcanoes.
> The salts and minerals it carries in solution.
> Its seasons, winds and weather, and
> the thousands of varieties of life it nourishes.

Countless men since Noah's time have known the sea intimately because they risked their lives to get their living from it. Science, however, had little understanding of the sea until a century ago. There was no pressing need; today there is.

The human population has outgrown its food supply and goes on multiplying with alarming speed. Yet man's living space remains the same—some 57 million square miles, a mere three tenths of the global surface. The other seven tenths, almost 145 million square miles, is water-surfaced. The ocean's life-supporting zones, beginning at the top, reach down for many thousand feet. And where there is life, there must be food for mankind. What oceanography, a teaming-up of older sciences, can teach may well decide the future of the human race. The oceans are the frontier that coming generations will explore and cultivate.

She felt herself to be in a better position to write about the sea than any writer could have been even a decade earlier. The study of oceans had leaped so far forward during World War II that scientists had learned more in those ten years than they had in the century before.

She received a contract early in May 1949, but contrary to her usual way of doing things, she failed to sign and return it for several weeks because she had mislaid it. She was too busy reading, organizing her information, corresponding with ocean scientists, and doing the actual writing. All this had to be done evenings and weekends because her days still belonged to the Fish and Wildlife Service.

Never having had any real underwater experiences, she agreed with Dr. William Beebe's affectionate admonition: "You can't write this book until you have gotten your head under water." She did. Though she swam like a beginner, she put on a diving helmet and explored, fifteen feet below the surface off the Florida coast in July 1949 and several times after that.

"You don't go very deep unless you are an experienced diver," she explained later. "I was a little nervous, too, because the mechanics are a bit involved for a novice. And the sound of air coming into the helmet is not very pleasant"—to say nothing of the lead weights on her feet. But at least she had been where the fishes were.

She and Mrs. Rodell became the first women to make a voyage on the *Albatross III,* the Fish and Wildlife survey ship. They spent a week cruising about George's Bank several hundred miles northeast of Cape Cod, most of the time in heavy fog. In the wheelhouse she listened through the hydrophones to the sounds of the North Atlantic's underwater tenants and watched the automatic depth recorders trace the ups and downs of the ocean floor. In the laboratory below deck she worked and talked with the ship's biologists as they examined specimens of the fish populations they caught with huge otter trawls. She also studied especially interesting forms of plankton —microscopic animal and vegetable life named from the Greek word for "wandering," because it drifts in huge clouds with the ocean currents. These countless billions of miniscule beings draw their nourishment directly from the minerals dissolved in seawater. Thus they become the first link in the species-eat-species food chain leading from the smallest of creatures to the 100-foot whale.

Rachel needed still more working time if she was to finish her manuscript in ten months, as she had promised. Luckily, in August 1949, she was granted a $2,250 fellowship by the Eugene F. Saxton Memorial, which often helped writers at work on difficult but unusually worthwhile projects. The money made it possible for her to take a leave without pay from her government job, beginning that October.

Almost at once, her life took on a kind of freedom it had never had before. She kept the same carefree hours as her cat, Muffin, working as late into the night and sleeping as late into the morning as she pleased. When Rachel was at work Muffin liked to cuff at the typewriter keyboard and watch the keys spring back. Rachel excused this behavior on the ground that the cat was helping her write.

Visiting Rachel at Silver Spring that fall, Vaudrin returned with the happy feeling that the book would succeed far beyond his first mildly optimistic guess of "four to six thousand copies." Enthusiasm began to build up in the Oxford Press offices.

The following spring Rachel and Vaudrin, first at lunch in New York, and then by mail, tried to choose a title. Their list included *The Book of the Ocean* and *Mother Sea*. So many ideas passed between them that when she suggested *The Sea Around Us* to Vaudrin, she did not remember whether they had already considered the title. Vaudrin wrote her: "I think we did. It has a nice sound and deserves to be put toward the top of the list."

Rachel delivered the manuscript of *The Sea Around Us* early in July 1950. It had been typed by her mother, whose hand and eye were as sure at eighty-one as they had been in earlier times. She told Vaudrin that she was pleased to let the book, at last, become his responsibility. Completion of *Under the Sea Wind* had left her empty of any eagerness to begin another book, she recalled. But now she could hardly wait to start her next one.

What Vaudrin recognized in those neatly typed pages was something more than a book. It was a working model of the seas, the continents, and their surrounding atmosphere, fashioned of words. Rachel's writing made the billion-year time-flow of the ocean's origin and history believable. Her words made visible the ocean's surface vastness, its miles-down depths, its awesome power expressed in tides and currents, winds and waves. Sea, earth, and atmosphere appeared as mighty forces that worked now in concert, now in conflict with each other—creating, nullifying, recreating environments for living matter.

The sea was the first of all environments. There life began in times unthinkably remote; there it flourishes today in marvelous varieties and numbers. Rachel returned often to this fact of the sea as "that great mother of life." But she wanted her readers to understand living matter, the waters, and the lands they embraced as inseparable parts of a universal wonder—the planet Earth. This second book, no less than her first, had a fine poetic quality but a quite different one. *Under the Sea Wind* was lyric. *The Sea Around Us* was epic.

Vaudrin's reading of the manuscript left him deeply satisfied. If he still wondered whether book buyers, after all, would spend $3.50 to find out how and why the sea was around them, he could find a clue in the last paragraph of Chapter I:

He [man] cannot control or change the ocean as, in his brief tenancy of earth, he has subdued and plundered the continents. In the artificial world of his cities and towns, he often forgets the true nature of his planet and the long vistas of its history, in which the existence of the race of men has occupied a mere moment of time. The sense of all these things comes to him most clearly in the course of a long ocean voyage, when he watches day after day the receding rim of the horizon, ridged and furrowed by waves; when at night he becomes aware of the earth's rotation as the stars pass overhead; or when, alone in this world of water and sky, he feels the loneliness of his earth in space. And then, as never on land, he knows the truth that his world is a water world, a planet dominated by its covering mantle of ocean, in which the continents are but transient intrusions of land above the surface of the all-encircling sea.

Good things began happening to the as-yet-unpublished *The Sea Around Us*. One of its chapters, "The Birth of an Island," appeared in the *Yale Review*. It won a $1,000 prize, the American Association for the Advancement of Science-George Westinghouse Award for the best science writing to appear in a magazine during 1950. Three days after Christmas Rachel was in Cleveland to accept the honor and the money at a luncheon assembly attended by several hundred writers, scientists, and newspaper reporters. Her shyness and her short supply of small talk for strangers made the occasion something of an inward agony. Yet, to the people she met there, she came through as a soft-spoken, bright, fortyish lady —conservatively groomed, altogether personable, and entirely self-possessed.

Then—1951. What a year *that* was.

In January Rachel visited Florida, just to keep in touch with the ocean, then returned to Silver Spring.

In February, she wrote to Margaret Nicholson, Oxford's chief copy editor, that she rather missed the familiar daily excitement of working on *The Sea Around Us*. She was waiting to hear from *The New Yorker*.

The excitement had only begun. What she heard from *The New Yorker*, a nationally important weekly, was an offer of several thousand dollars for the right to reprint parts of the book. They would appear as a "biography" of the ocean in the magazine's "Profile" department, which was usually devoted to the life stories of remarkable individuals. Some of Rachel's friends who knew little about publishing asked, "If the magazine prints so much of it, won't that keep people from buying the book?" She and Marie Rodell were sure the exact opposite would be true. It was.

In May *Nature Magazine* published a chapter from *The Sea Around Us*. And *Reader's Digest* was offering $10,000 for the right to reprint the book in cut-down form as one of its regular "Condensation from the Book" features.

An explosive kind of literary excitement was beginning to build up around this quiet little government employee who lived with her mother and kept a cat. To the Oxford people it seemed quite clear that Miss Carson was about to be recognized as one of the most remarkable writers of her generation. Her special talent was that she could reveal the beauty as well as the straightforward aspects of a single fact, a small pattern of facts, and the whole vast complicated system of facts that makes the natural world what it is. More successfully than many writers before her, she broke through the dullness barrier of science writing for the large mass of nonscientific readers.

Neither Oxford nor Rachel, however, could have separated their sense of literary achievement from the commercial success it promised. Publishers, after all, were in business to make money. And for the first time in Rachel's life it seemed possible that her earn-

ings would allow her to become a full-time, independent writer, free to make her own choices about
where, when, and what to write. Since that's what was
happening, and the whole Oxford organization was
pitching in to help it along, Rachel realized reluc-
tantly that she had to help, too.

Despite her dislike for being in the public eye, she
was the guest of honor at a reception arranged by Oxford at the National Press Club in June. Book reviewers, magazine editors, newspaper people, and
government officials attended. She couldn't believe
such an event was real but she knew her writing was.
Remembering the long sections of her book *The
New Yorker* had just printed, she found it easier to
believe that she had a reason for being there. She
charmed everyone by being simply herself. When it
was over, she went to Beaufort, North Carolina, for a
week of scientific and literary beachcombing.

Before she left there was something she had to do.
Two or three times a week for many months while
she was working on the book, Bob Hines had carried
heavy armloads of reference materials from the Department of the Interior library to her waiting
Chevvy. He had carried them again on the return
trip. Now Rachel paid a call on him and handed him
an advance copy of *The Sea Around Us*. She had written in it: "To Bob Hines, who bore many of the
burdens connected with the writing of this book."

The nationwide Rachel Carson explosion was
touched off on July 2, the day *The Sea Around Us*
was officially offered to the public. It was also an-

nounced as a Book-of-the-Month Club selection. Before the end of the month, it was on *The New York Times*'s best-seller list. It remained there for eighty-one weeks.

If a really unfavorable review of the book was ever published, it has not come to light. The coolest of the reviewers were merely enthusiastic. From the warmest ones there was an endless chorus of praise. They hailed her writing style for its simplicity, rhythm, and sweeping force. One critic wrote, and most others agreed, that "Miss Carson happens to be one of those very rare scientists who can also write magnificently."

Though Rachel had to admit this was *her* explosion, it was just too much. She went to Bar Harbor, Maine, then headed south to spend August at Woods Hole. Both places had miles-long sea edges, quietly teeming with life, which she wanted to explore anew.

She was able to spend the first two fall months working in her study at Silver Spring, except for an October interruption to address a Book and Author Luncheon in New York. She felt like running for her life when she found herself facing an audience of 1,500. As part of her talk she played a recording of undersea sounds—the clicking of shrimp and the squeaking of dolphins.

In November she had to appear in the book department of Cleveland's best-known department store, Halle's, to present the 100,000th copy of her book to one shopper; then she signed copies for dozens of others who were eager to see the writer of the book they had just bought. Whatever she felt about being on display in the huge store, she was rewarded by the beginning of a fine personal friendship with Dr. George Crile, Jr., and his wife, the former Jane Halle. Dr. Crile, one of the world's leading cancer specialists, was also an amateur explorer and underwater photographer who had a special appreciation for Rachel's writings about the sea. Mrs. Crile, a member of the family that founded the store, discovered that she and Rachel had many mutual acquaintances in Washington.

The next day Rachel was in Pittsburgh, autographing more copies for the customers at Gimbel's. Again she was inwardly uncomfortable, but since Pittsburgh, of all places, chose to look at her admiringly, she responded graciously.

Ruth Swisshelm, a classmate who had become an official of Chatham College, made the trip downtown from its northern height. She said hello and kept Rachel company for half an hour.

"When students brought her books to sign she brightened up. When Chatham students came, she brightened even more. For them she wrote more than just her name."

December had its own quota of triumphs and distractions. RCA-Victor released a new symphonic album, Debussy's *La Mer* ("The Sea") conducted by Arturo Toscanini, with a commentary written by Rachel. She made superb use of her scientist-poet's talent to explain "the shining beauty, the awful power, and the eternal mystery of the sea" that can be heard in *La Mer*. She knew how to listen to music as well as to the sounds of nature.

RKO Studios was negotiating for the right to make a feature-length documentary film of *The Sea Around Us* in technicolor. The women's-page editors of the nation's newspapers voted Rachel "Woman of the Year in Literature."

She was achieving the kind of literary success her college classmates freely predicted for her, with a far different kind of book than she or they had imagined. But in the deepest layers of her satisfaction there was something else—the friendships she had made among the world fraternity of marine scientists who are united rather than separated by the oceans. They saw the seas and all of nature with much the same eyes as she did. Their approval of her work made her their unofficial spokeswoman, in a sense, to the larger, non-scientific world. There was, for instance, Henry Bryant Bigelow, marine zoologist and oceanographer who had worked at Harvard University for several decades and had been director of the Woods Hole Oceanographic Institution. Of him Rachel wrote: "Bigelow is probably the best-known and most beloved figure in oceanography the world over, and he has been extraordinarily good to me."

Then there was the letter she had received from Gustaf Arrhenius, one of Sweden's leading marine scientists:

. . . before having seen your book I was somewhat skeptical because I have never before seen any successful popular treatment of this subject, or rather, this immense amount of subjects. But unluckily enough, I started to read it; unluckily because I

> have some very urgent work just at this moment
> and once I started with your book I couldn't possi-
> bly finish [my work], that fascinating did I find it
> from the first page to the last . . . . I felt obliged
> to write to you to express my admiration . . . .
> Again, congratulations to your masterpiece.

She could ask for nothing more, except release
from her activities as a celebrity. The demands on her
time and energy were beginning to get her down, she
wrote to Fon Boardman, Oxford's vice-president in
charge of advertising and promotion. To meet more
than a small, carefully selected number of them, she
said, would require a kind of chaos that could be du-
plicated only in the pages of *Alice in Wonderland.*

Just the same she went to Philadelphia, in January
1952, to accept the Henry G. Bryant medal of the
Philadelphia Geographical Society, the first ever con-
ferred on a woman. At the end of the month she was in
New York to receive the gold medallion of the National Book Award for the best nonfiction book of
1951. In her formal acceptance speech she said:

> Many people have commented with surprise on
> the fact that a work of science should have a large
> popular sale . . . . We live in a scientific age
> . . . . The materials of science are the materials of
> life itself. Science is part of the reality of living; it is
> the what, the how, and the why of everything in our
> experience . . . . If there is poetry in my book
> about the sea, it is not because I deliberately put it

there but because no one could write truthfully about the sea and leave out the poetry.

Late in spring she traveled again, to accept three honorary degrees: Doctor of Letters from Drexel Institute of Technology in Philadelphia; Doctor of Science from Oberlin College in Oberlin, Ohio; and Doctor of Literature from her alma mater, Chatham College. (The following year she was made an honorary Doctor of Literature by Smith College in Northampton, Massachusetts.)

At Chatham, Rachel stood with her classmate, Ruth Swisshelm, in the receiving line to greet guests at an alumnae tea. She looked a little uncomfortable.

"Are you all right?" Mrs. Swisshelm asked.

"The truth is," Rachel smiled ruefully, "I'm much more at home barefoot in the sand or on shipboard in sneakers than on hardwood floors in high heels."

NORTH IN SUMMER

Sea of stretch'd ground-swells!
Sea breathing broad and convulsive
*   breaths!*
Sea of the brine of Life! . . .
I am integral with you—I too am of
*   one phase, and of all phases.*

            —WALT WHITMAN

Summer found Rachel sneakered and very much at home on the Maine seacoast. Keeping house with her mother in a rented cottage she began the realization of a long-delayed dream. She bought a one-and-a-half-acre patch of land at West Southport, along the west shore of Boothbay Harbor. On her first visit many years before, she had fallen in love with this rugged region where tall trees look over the edges of cliffs at the sea-scarred, solid-rock face of the beach below. That's where her house would be, close to the edge of such a cliff. Every room would have windows from which one could see great stretches of sky and water, their changing moods and colors, and the swift powerful movement of the tides. She knew now, like Silverbar, her sanderling in *Under the Sea Wind*, where her northward flights would bring her the next summer, and the next, and the next . . .

This was also the time and the place to dig into a long-delayed writing project. Shortly after she finished *The Sea Around Us,* the publishing firm of Houghton Mifflin had asked her to write "a guide to the life of the shore" for its nature guide series. Since courtesy and a clause in Rachel's contract made it necessary to ask Oxford's consent, Mrs. Rodell discussed the matter with Philip Vaudrin.

The editor agreed but said he hoped Rachel would remain an Oxford author except for that one book. Much would depend, Mrs. Rodell replied, on whether she could get a publisher to put out a new edition of *Under the Sea Wind.* Vaudrin thought the book certainly deserved another chance. "It contains the finest writing on ocean life that one could hope to find nowadays," he wrote in a memo to the company's chief executive. But months went by while Oxford and Mrs. Rodell negotiated.

Meanwhile Rachel started planning her book. She had no intention of producing merely another illustrated catalog of the shore's plant and animal life. There were plenty of those. Besides, there wasn't much point in being able to tell the difference in looks between a fiddler crab and a calico crab if you didn't know how different their lives were, and why. She decided to use an ecological approach, describing each plant or animal as a member of a particular kind of shore community, in the tidal zone, above it, or below.

It would be a painstaking, time-consuming piece of work, which she could not accomplish unless she got a year's leave without pay from her government job. Albert M. Day, director of the Fish and Wildlife Service, agreed to this unusually long absence because he understood the need for such a book. But what would Rachel do for money? In November 1950 she was not yet able to guess how much *The Sea Around Us* would begin earning six months later. From North Carolina, where she had gone to recover from an operation, she wrote to the John S. Guggenheim Foundation, asking for funds to support her work. In April 1951 she was granted a working fellowship and $4,000. She began her year's government leave in June, the very month of "the Rachel Carson explosion." She was too busy to do much work on her shore guide the rest of that year, or even to wonder what Oxford was doing about reissuing *Under the Sea Wind*. She was happily exploring a southern beach when the new edition of her first book appeared in April 1952. It was an immediate success. Like *The Sea Around Us,* it became a Book-of-the-Month Club offering. For months thereafter Rachel Carson had two books on the weekly best-seller lists, something that happens to very few authors.

This time the reviews were not merely appreciative but highly enthusiastic. Sterling North, one of the nation's most widely published book reviewers, wrote: *"Under the Sea Wind* is comparable in every way to *The Sea Around Us* . . . . Once again we have a book from a mind able to fuse poetry and science into that rare commodity known as literature."

Harvey Breit in *The New York Times* said: "Its

pages reveal the identical gifts that today have capti-
vated readers: a scrupulous scholarship, a firsthand,
warm, individual knowledge of the ocean, and a
poetic sensibility."

The comment that may well have given Rachel,
Marie Rodell, and Oxford the greatest satisfaction
came from Alfred C. Ames in the *Chicago Tribune:*
"The author of *The Sea Around Us* has not done it
again; rather, she had done it before, in 1941, with
the original publication of *Under the Sea Wind.* The
book, which then was a volume by a commercially
obscure author . . . is now reissued in the expecta-
tion of triumph . . . *Under the Sea Wind* deserves
to triumph. It has the clearness and the depth of un-
contaminated ocean water."

Reading the 1952 reviews, Rachel could only
shrug her shoulders and reflect on a familiar irony:
Literary fame and literary merit do not always, and
perhaps not very often, go together. If her second
book had not been a huge commercial success, her
first one might never have been read again. How
clever and businesslike it had been of Marie Rodell
to press for re-publication. Rachel, however, was no
respecter of best-seller lists. She admired or disliked
no book for its reputation but only for what she herself found in its pages. Neither was she dazzled by the
large sums of money her long-neglected book was
now earning. Though she had always needed money
she had never lusted after it. She was fiercely pleased
because at last justice was being done to *Under the
Sea Wind.* Warmed by her triumph and reddened by

the Florida sun, Rachel returned to Washington and resigned from the Fish and Wildlife Service.

Two years had gone by since Houghton Mifflin had first asked her to write the seashore guide which was eventually published as *The Edge of the Sea.* Now she could get on with it. At her suggestion the publisher offered Bob Hines a contract as illustrator. Hines the artist and Carson the writer made a great team. Each understood and sympathized with what the other was trying to do. They agreed that most of the drawings should be made from live specimens collected on location. If that meant going to the Florida Keys, the North Carolina beaches, Cape Cod, and the Maine coast, so much the better. Hines had a protective "big brother" attitude toward Rachel. She needed somebody to look after her when she really got wrapped up in her field work.

In Florida he had to carry her out of a mangrove swamp because she had stayed until she was bone-tired and couldn't move. Nor did she notice, as she roamed long hours on the tidal flats wearing a bathing suit, that squadrons of mosquitoes were feasting on her. Half a dozen times at Boothbay Harbor, Hines lifted the frail, small-boned writer out of barnacle-covered tide pools.

"She was frozen," he said. "She just couldn't get out by herself. If you slip in those pools you come out a mass of cuts and scratches. I've seen her get into one of them when the tide was going out and stay there until the tide came in again. That's a darn long time to stay in Maine ocean water."

Much of it was easier, from Hines' descriptions: "We'd go out on the mud flats. She'd scrounge around to find what she wanted. We'd bring the stuff back in a bucket and I'd make the drawings. Then Rachel would put them back in the bucket and return them to their natural places on the beach."

Hines was good company. Unable to remember the scientific name of whatever small animal he was drawing, he would call it a "wee beast" for convenience. Rachel was amused, and "wee beast" became part of their working vocabulary. Hines—a man of warm, outgoing personality—could make her laugh, not by being deliberately funny but by the quality of his conversation. None of it ever had to do with big jokes.

Hines said, thinking about the years they worked together on the book: "She had a subdued sense of humor. The impression of her laughter is more vivid than any detail of its causes. They were small un-memorable things. All I can remember is her beauti-ful tinkling laugh in moments when she felt strongly the enjoyment of being alive. It was good to hear her laugh."

In Maine there was more laughter than elsewhere. She found warm friends there. Stanley and Dorothy Freeman, a Massachusetts couple who had a summer cottage on Dogfish Head, half a mile down the shore, had read *The Sea Around Us* with quiet joy. Here, at last, was a writer who succeeded in saying what they had long felt. When the *Boothbay Register* reported that Rachel Carson was building a house nearby, they sent her a welcoming note. She was charmed by its informal, friendly, yet dignified tone. At Christmas she replied that she would like to call on them the following summer. She did.

The Freemans were as good in person as they seemed on paper. They were not the kind of city people who came just "to get away from it all." They were bound by deep feelings to this meeting place of forest, sky, and water. Dorothy had worked for the Extension Service of the Department of Agriculture and had been Massachusetts leader of 4-H Club work for girls. Stanley was a specialist in agricultural problems for a Massachusetts feed company, and a highly capable amateur photographer and small-boat sailor. When the Freemans weren't in Maine they lived in West Bridgewater, Massachusetts.

Between Rachel and the Freemans there quickly developed a feeling of closeness such as the lifelong "loner" had seldom experienced. She could talk freely to them about the problems and progress of her work on the book.

Her first chapter was "a series of recollections of places that have stirred me deeply." In it she expressed "some of the thoughts and feelings that make the sea's edge, for me, a place of exceeding beauty and fascination."

Dorothy Freeman, who had walked these beaches all her life, guided her to one such place. It was a tide pool in a small marine fairyland—a cave whose entrance was well above water only during the year's lowest tides. Even then it was too small to admit a

person. Rachel clambered to the cave's broad rock
sill, kneeled and sprawled on its slippery carpeting of
wet sea moss, looked, and remembered. Not so much
because she was collecting material for her book, but
because nature had allowed her to peek at one of its
small yet wonderful secrets.

> The floor of the cave was only a few inches below
> the roof [she wrote in *The Edge of the Sea*], and a
> mirror had been created in which all that grew on
> the ceiling was reflected in the still water below
> . . . . In the moment when I looked into the cave a
> little elfin starfish hung down, suspended by the
> merest thread, perhaps only by a single tube foot. It
> reached down to touch its own reflection . . . .

Stanley, taking his turn on the ledge, managed to
make some color photographs of the dangling "wee
beast."

It was a good summer and so were those that followed. When the tide was right, Rachel went down to
the beach carrying a bucket and wearing a biologist's
belt loaded with specimen bottles. At her worktable
she would study her finds under a magnifying glass or
through her powerful binocular microscope.

She went on beach picnics with her mother, the
Freemans, and Bob Hines. Once in a while she went
sailing with the Freemans in their sixteen-foot sloop,
"more to please us than because she wanted to.
Rachel was a little edgy in a small boat." The more so
because once Stanley, maneuvering his craft to give

Rachel an offshore view of her house, managed to crunch onto some tide-covered rocks.

Often Rachel and her mother would go down the steep wooden stairway from the house to the beach for a gull-feeding break. Rachel would swing a food-filled paper bag in long slow circles. The gulls would close in and take pieces of bread from her hand. There was a friendly neighborhood squirrel who didn't mind sitting in her lap when she had goodies to feed him. And there was Jeffy, the cat. Once Rachel's mother disposed of his leftover food by making cat-food sandwiches for the gulls.

Far out from the foot of the cliff on which the Free-mans' house sat, the sea, over thousands of years, had scooped a large tide pool of egg-shaped outline in beach rock. On clear nights Rachel and the Freemans sometimes sat on the seaward verandah to watch the moon. They would follow its steady progress as it lighted point after point along the water. When at last the moon could see itself reflected in the tide pool, they would applaud. It was wise and knowing applause, the kind one would expect of an audience sophisticated enough to attend this theater of celestial happenings.

Rachel lingered well into the fall, wanting never to leave. She missed the Freemans, who had gone back earlier, as though she had known them years instead of weeks. But she took joy in the company she brought back to the house from her beach visits at the lowest low tides.

She thought it paradise enough to find thirty big

anemones, six to eight inches long, under one tide-pool ledge. A small specimen broken from the beach rock was entertainment for a whole evening. It was pink coralline algae thickly covering some empty barnacle shells. At her worktable she found in this lit-tle mass of sea stuff a tiny world silently simmering with a dozen varieties of life. Within the empty barnacle shells tiny anemones were feeding madly. A new generation of baby barnacles was coming along quite nicely. And under the microscope she looked at *Spirorbis borealis,* a tiny plumed worm who fastens its pinhead-sized, snail-like shell to rocks or seaweed. Rachel, like most marine zoologists, was endlessly fascinated by its beauty. The thick layer of algae was shot through with tunnels made by tiny crustaceans. Sometimes one of them would stick its head out, and its single glowing eye would remind Rachel of a miner wearing his lighted head lamp.

After "lights out" she listened to the rough, sweet lullaby of the surf beyond the windows of her moon-brightened bedroom, wondering sleepily what fasci-nations the shore and its creatures would offer her in the course of another day.

There was one thing she didn't enjoy that summer, the RKO company's film of *The Sea Around Us.*

She told Dorothy Freeman of her distaste for the film version of the book saying that, however, if Dorothy insisted on seeing it, she would not hold it against her. She was pleased that the *Washington Post,* while speaking favorably of some of the photog-raphy, had severely criticized the script. Neverthe-

less, the film won an "Oscar" as the best feature-
length documentary for 1953.

Rachel returned to Silver Spring late in October.
At the end of December she attended the annual
meeting of the American Association for the Advancement of Science in Boston, where she read a
paper on "The Edge of the Sea." Then, home again to
wait out the dreary months that stood between her
and another season in Maine.

She spent much of her 1954 summer preparing an
illustrated lecture on seashore life to be delivered before the Audubon Society in Washington that fall.
Stanley Freeman worked for weeks making color
photographs for the slides she intended to show. The
demand for tickets was so great that she had to give
both a matinee and an evening performance. It was a
highly successful event, in which Stanley's pictures
played a featured role.

Rachel couldn't be offhand about such matters.
She had worked just as hard writing her lecture for
the benefit of the Lincoln County (Maine) Historical
Society in the Wiscasset high school gym a few
months earlier. The Wiscasset talk set some sort of a
local record for ticket sales—$1,000, which bought
new heating equipment for the society's building.

The Edge of the Sea was published in the fall of
1955. Like Rachel's two earlier books, it was very successful. There was a two-part "Profile" in *The New
Yorker* before publication and a long "Condensation
from the Book" in *Reader's Digest* a few months later.
It stayed on *The New York Times*'s best-seller list
for twenty-three weeks.

She had never meant it to be a guidebook of the ordinary kind, with plants and animals alphabetically listed and described. It wasn't, as her preface made clear:

> To understand the shore, it is not enough to catalogue its life. Understanding comes only when, standing on a beach, we can sense the long rhythms of earth and sea that sculptured its land forms and produced the rock and sand of which it is composed; when we can sense with the eye and ear of the mind the surge of life beating at its shores . . . . It is not enough to pick up an empty shell and say "This is a murex" and "That is an angel wing." True understanding demands intuitive comprehension of the whole life of the creature that once inhabited the empty shell . . . .

For Rachel Carson it was not enough to give her readers understanding without trying to make them feel at least a little of what she felt: "The shore is an ancient world . . . . Each time I enter it, I gain some new awareness of its beauty and its deeper meanings, sensing the intricate fabric of life by which one creature is linked with another, and each with its surroundings." Rachel wanted readers to feel something about the wonder of the world's oceans as a place where life is "a force as tangible as any of the physical realities of the sea, a force strong and purposeful, as incapable of being crushed or diverted from its end as the rising tide."

The comments of critics and reviewers across the country assured her that in this respect, too, she had been highly successful. Robert Cushman Murphy, a leading authority on the oceans' life, wrote: "A large and appreciative public awaits the present book for reasons of enjoyment no less than as education in one of the most fascinating but least known realms of natural history."

The Atlantic Monthly, which had published Rachel's first serious writing eighteen years earlier, commented: "It is a truly extraordinary world which Miss Carson vividly unfolds for us and which is admirably illustrated in Bob Hines' drawings."

The *Christian Science Monitor*'s reviewer wrote: "Miss Carson's pen is as poetic as ever and the knowledge she imparts is profound. *The Edge of the Sea* finds a worthy place beside Miss Carson's masterpiece of 1951."

Rachel was happier that year than she had ever been in her not-always-happy life. And she could look back at the years she gave to *The Edge of the Sea* as happy ones, too. In the long drudgery of her first two books she had found that writing was a lonely job. This one gave her a generous measure of companionship with three close friends. Bob Hines was present on page after page, with 160 illustrations. For the other two friends she had lovingly saved one special page. The book was dedicated, "To Dorothy and Stanley Freeman, who have gone down with me into the low-tide world and have felt its beauty and mystery."

SEVEN DEAD ROBINS

It is those who have compassion for all life who will best safeguard the life of man. Those who become aroused only when man is endangered become aroused too late.

—EDWIN WAY TEALE

At forty-eight, Rachel Carson occupied a prosperous, highly respected place in the world of literature and science thanks to three fairly small books of remarkable merit.

It had not been easy, of course. Yet she would have raised her thin, delicately arched eyebrows at the suggestion that life had in any way shortchanged her. True, she was unmarried. She confided to a friend that she would have liked to marry. Yet she never spoke of any one man she might have chosen. Many of the Fish and Wildlife men regarded her as attractive. She enjoyed their company at work, during lunch hours when they ate their sandwiches in a nearby park, and at occasional staff picnics on the Potomac River. She did nothing, however, to encourage anyone's romantic interest in her.

At best, the 1930's were not good marrying years for young men because so many of them just couldn't afford it. The World War II years were not good ones for women because men were scarce, especially in Washington.

In her preface to *The Edge of the Sea* Rachel wrote: "I have tried to interpret the shore in terms of that essential unity that binds life to the earth." She interpreted her own existence in terms of a unity that bound her to others. Neither absence, distance, nor the urgency of her own affairs could diminish her intense loyalty to friends. There was a day in 1950, for example, when Rachel got word that Mary Skinker was dying of cancer. She was pressed for time to finish *The Sea Around Us* and short of money, but she borrowed plane fare and flew to Chicago to be at Miss Skinker's bedside.

Besides, Rachel did have family ties of her own. Her nieces, Virginia and Marjorie Williams, were grown and married. Marjorie had a little boy who was old enough to want *Peter Rabbit* and other Beatrix Potter books read to him. The books were presents from Rachel, of course. Her feelings of responsibility and affection for her nieces had grown through the years until she was as much a mother as an aunt to them. But almost from the time of his birth, she felt especially drawn toward her small grandnephew. The infant Roger Christie, struggling to grow into his world, stirred her more deeply than any new-hatched Scomber the Mackerel she could ever invent. How much there was for this human newcomer to learn, and do, and love!

One autumn night in Maine Rachel wrapped twenty-month-old Roger in a blanket and carried him down to the beach to meet the ocean. It was the first of many such wanderings and explorations on which she and Roger went together. She knew that "a child's world is fresh and new and beautiful." She took tender satisfaction in helping Roger find that world, as Mother Carson had helped her.

Walking with Roger along the beaches and through the woods of Maine became an established part of her life. She would have found it painful to give up this new excitement of helping a child discover nature and of looking through his eyes, afresh, at long-familiar things. It was a very personal experience but it begged to become a public one. In the summer of 1955 she wrote the first long section of a new book about the small adventures she and Roger shared as explorers of their outdoor surroundings in Maine and Maryland. She began by telling of the night she brought Roger down to the rocky beach below her house:

> Out there, just at the edge of where-we-couldn't-see, big waves were thundering in, dimly seen white shapes that boomed and threw great handfuls of froth at us. Together we laughed for pure joy—he a baby meeting for the first time the wild tumult of Oceanus, I with the salt of half a lifetime of sea love in me.

Before he was two, Roger could tell a whelk, a periwinkle, or a mussel when he saw one, and speak their names imperfectly. But that was not the point.

It is possible to compile extensive lists of creatures seen and identified [Rachel wrote] without having once caught a breath-taking glimpse of the wonder of life. If a child asked me a question that suggested even a faint awareness of the mystery behind the arrival of a migrant sandpiper on the beach of an August morning, I would be far more pleased . . . .

What she wrote that summer appeared the following summer in a major magazine, *Woman's Home Companion,* under the title, "Help Your Child to Wonder." Then more urgent literary and personal matters thrust themselves into her life and she could find no time to add to the article. It was published in book form ten years later as *The Sense of Wonder,* with color photographs by Charles Pratt and others. Many of Pratt's pictures were made near Rachel's house in Maine, along the beach, and in the woods. All of them were faithful to the blend of poetry and science that made Rachel so rare a writer.

The most carefree period of Rachel's life came to a sudden halt at the beginning of 1957. Marjorie, long in delicate health, died of a respiratory ailment. Rachel adopted five-year-old Roger and he became her son by law. Mother Carson was infirm and she needed looking after. Rachel was also obliged to supervise the contractors who were building a new house for her in Silver Spring. She was tired. She had colds. She lost some weight. Moving into the new house in March was a less joyous occasion than she had dreamed it would be. She was spending much less time than she wanted in her spacious new book-lined study. Roger's welfare, because he was young, and her mother's, because she was now eighty-nine, made daily demands on Rachel's time and attention.

Nevertheless she welcomed an invitation from Harper & Brothers to do a book for their World Perspectives series. She felt she had written herself out of the ocean. Now she intended to write about the continents as she had about the seas—a book that might be called *Remembrances of Earth.* She never got around to it.

A letter Rachel received in January 1958 changed her plans. It came from Olga Owens Huckins, book editor of *The Boston Post,* a resident of Duxbury, Massachusetts, and Rachel's friend of six years' standing:

> The mosquito control plane flew over our small town last summer. Since we live close to the marshes we were treated to several lethal doses, as the pilot criss-crossed over our place . . . . We consider the spraying of active poison over private land to be a serious aerial intrusion.
>
> The "harmless" shower bath killed seven of our lovely song-birds outright. We picked up three dead bodies the next morning, right by the door . . . . The next day three were scattered around the bird bath. I had emptied it and scrubbed it after the spraying, but YOU CAN NEVER KILL DDT. On the following day one robin dropped suddenly from a branch in our woods.

We were too heart-sick to hunt for other corpses. All of these birds died horribly, and in the same way. Their bills were gaping open and their splayed claws were drawn up to their breasts in agony.

Air spraying where it is not needed or wanted is inhuman, undemocratic, and probably unconstitutional. For those of us who stand helplessly on the tortured earth, it is intolerable.

Reading the letter, Rachel decided to postpone her book about the earth's billions-of-years-old past. Her readers needed, much more urgently, to think about its future. Her tiredness fell away from her.

A QUESTION FOR
HOMO SAPIENS

Man has inherited the earth . . . .
For the first time in the history of the
planet a single species dominates all
. . . and the shambles is evident.

—N. J. BERRILL

Olga Huckins' phrase, the tortured earth, lit the slow-burning fuse of a second "Carson explosion" that would make the earlier one seem like a damp fire-cracker.

Books and her own eyes had taught Rachel that the tortures of the earth were many:

Mountainsides shorn of trees, then washed bedrock-bare because no living tree roots held the soil.

Lush Appalachian country turned to ashen moon-scapes, the surface life stripped off by power shovels at sixty tons per bite, to reach the coal just underneath.

Salt marshes filled, their tidal life destroyed, for real-estate promotions.

Farmlands worked to death, then put to work

again with mineral transfusions of phosphate, lime, and nitrogen.

These were long familiar. New ones had been added in her lifetime:

Radioactive test-bomb ashes lingering on, above, and underneath the ground. Wastes from nuclear reactors used for peaceful purposes sloshing in sealed containers on the ocean floors, where—it was merely hoped—they would be harmless.

Sewage, chemical sludge, and solid trash pouring into lakes and rivers.

Carbon monoxide fumes rising from several hundred million buses, trucks, and autos, from farm machinery, suburban snowplows, golf carts, garden mowers, outboard motors, to mingle with the sulfurous breath of countless chimneys.

These and dozens more together were the new, most modern tortures of the earth—pollution. Pollution not merely of a lake, a beach, a river, here and there; but of entire river systems, of air across wide regions, of coastlines by the hundred miles, and of the sea itself where rivers, dirtied even at their sources, come down to it.

DDT, the stuff that poisoned Olga Huckins' birds, and its chemical relatives were rapidly becoming the world's most widespread, dangerous pollutants. They were the inventions of chemists who used the remarkable ability of the carbon atom to combine with atoms of other elements, such as hydrogen, chlorine, and phosphorus. By arranging and rearranging such atoms, chemists were able to invent new types of chemicals. Two of these types, chlorinated hydrocarbons and organic phosphates, became known as synthetic pesticides. Separately they were known by many other names: aldrin, benzine hexachloride, chlordane, dieldrin, heptachlor, lindane, malathion, parathion, 2,4-D. They were not intended to pollute the earth, of course, but to kill crop-damaging and disease-carrying insects, funguses, weeds, and small animals.

DDT (dichloro-diphenyl-trichloro-ethane) was first known in 1874, but its uses as a pesticide were not discovered until 1939, when it saved a Swiss potato crop from the Colorado beetle, which had spread from the Rocky Mountains to Europe fifty years earlier. Its reputation grew during World War II because it prevented a deadly typhus epidemic in Italy. Used as a dusting powder, it killed body lice that carried the disease. In the years right after the war, more than two hundred such basic chemicals were developed. DDT and its relatives quickly showed themselves to be great savers of time, money, and labor. Their magic was proclaimed in millions of dollars' worth of paid advertising and in radio and television broadcasts, magazine articles, and newspaper stories. The headlines imitated the style of the war news Americans had become accustomed to reading:

WAR ON INSECTS
CHEMICAL MARVELS TAKE THE BUGS
OUT OF LIVING
MORE BUG-KILLING POWER
BAD NEWS FOR BUGS.

Since 1945, billions of pounds of these materials, sold under several thousand brand names, had been spread hundreds of thousands of square miles across America's face. As much as half a billion pounds were being added yearly. Farmers, dairymen, foresters, and even housewives and home gardeners were buying them eagerly.

Bad news for bugs was not entirely good news for people. Biologists, medical experts, and wildlife specialists—Rachel Carson among them—realized that these pesticides held hidden, delayed-action dangers. Rachel had first made the acquaintance of these materials in reports from government biologists and independent scientists during her Fish and Wildlife days. As far back as 1946 Elmer Higgins and Clarence Cottam, in the *Journal of Economic Entomology*, had written about DDT as a threat to mammals, birds, and fish.

In the years that followed, scientific evidence of the dangers continued to pile up. Reports of fish kills were becoming so numerous that in 1958 Congress ordered the Department of the Interior to study the effects of pesticides on fish and wildlife. Two years later the government started an annual census of fish killed by various kinds of pollution. Each report had numerous items such as this:

"Careless handling and spraying of pesticide (Ethion) during summer spraying of orange groves surrounding a lake resulted in 61,745 fish being killed."

"Cotton fields sprayed with one and one-half pints

per acre of endrin and methyl parathion once a week by airplane. Some 71,430 fish killed following heavy local rains which washed poison into creek."

Yet most people knew almost nothing about this darker side of the picture because very little of it was appearing in the newspapers and magazines. Overwhelmed by the campaign in praise of pesticides, the general public knew and cared only about the quick, money-in-the-bank, trouble-saving benefits.

It was a complicated subject, even for Rachel. During most of 1958 she spent hundreds of eye-straining hours reading and digesting the large mass of material she had collected. In December her life and her work suffered a sad, inevitable interruption.

Maria Carson died six months short of her ninetieth birthday. She had lived the last years of her life happily in the bright shadow of her daughter's fame. Sometimes she had gone with her on short trips along the Maine seacoast. While Rachel explored rocky, slippery beaches, Mrs. Carson sat in the family car writing letters. To passersby who showed any inclination to stop and chat for a moment, she would say, pointing, "That's my daughter, Rachel Carson. She wrote *The Sea Around Us*." Now, Rachel, accepting her loss, found comfort in young Roger's company and went back to work, only to face a new interruption.

The Oxford University Press wanted her to enlarge and revise *The Sea Around Us* for a new edition. Oceanography had made such great advances in less than ten years that her manuscript needed to be brought up to date. Nobody knew that better than she, but what about the pesticide book? She held off Oxford as long as she was able. Then she decided she would have to ride two horses at once, somehow.

For the next year Rachel worked on both books. She had always been a slow, careful writer, but everything seemed slower and harder than she could ever remember. She woke up almost as tired as she went to bed. At her desk, she shook off the feeling and strengthened herself with thoughts of the coming months in Maine. The summer magic of north-country sea and earth always made her feel better. But when she returned to Silver Spring in autumn, weariness reentered her days. Her revisions of *The Sea Around Us* were still unfinished. To make better use of her time, she hired an assistant. Jeanne Davis, with experience on several scientific journals, became her secretary and research aide. They worked well together and they liked each other. But Rachel, though she now accomplished more, continued to feel fatigued.

Early in the spring of 1960 she went to a Washington physician for a checkup. The doctor found a cancerous growth in one of her breasts. The first week in April she underwent surgery. After long weeks of recovery, she moved to Maine again for the summer.

How many more summers might there be for her? Many? Few? . . . None? This was no time for self-pitying, fright-ridden guessing games. She had work to do against a deadline not marked on any calendar but hidden in the life processes of her own perishable body. Her doctors would make the best guesses and take the wisest steps they could. She would be *their* responsibility. Hers was to get on with the job.

She gave most of her time and energy to the pesticide book but managed to finish her revisions of *The Sea Around Us* in October. Her preface to the new edition was a stern warning against pollution of the oceans by the dumping of atomic radioactive wastes. Oceanographers, she explained, now knew that the deepest waters and the ocean floor itself were not eternally motionless. On the contrary they were powerfully in motion over vast areas. These findings were making science aware of a world threat at least as serious as pollution by pesticides.

> In unlocking the secrets of the atom [Rachel wrote], man has found himself confronted with a frightening problem—what to do with the most dangerous materials that have ever existed in all the earth's history, the by-products of atomic fission. The stark problem that faces him is whether he can dispose of these lethal substances without rendering the earth uninhabitable . . . . No account of the sea today is complete unless it takes note of this ominous problem.

There was a terrible lack of knowledge about what these atomic wastes might be doing to the waters, floors, and life forms of the oceans. Tests did show, however, that the sealed, concrete-lined barrels of atomic rubbish, sunk deep enough, could be smashed by the ocean's pressure. Yet, as in the use of pesticides, very little information about the dangers was being given to the public.

> The truth is [Rachel concluded] that disposal has proceeded far more rapidly than our knowledge justifies. To dispose first and investigate later is an invitation to disaster, for once radioactive elements have been deposited at sea they are irretrievable. The mistakes made now are made for all time.

Her last paragraph was a sigh of deep sorrow for the recklessness with which modern man was using his godlike scientific abilities:

> It is a curious situation that the sea, from which all life first arose, should now be threatened by one form of that life. But the sea, though changed in a sinister way, will continue to exist; the threat is rather to life itself.

Now she could give full attention and energy once more to her warning against pollution of the earth. The pattern of what she wanted to say and how she wanted to say it began to take its final shape on paper.

The new pesticides were super-poisons. They could kill by skin contact as well as by being inhaled or swallowed. A tank-truck driver died the day after plunging his arm into a drum of pentachlorophenol to find an object he had dropped.

The pesticides killed good insects, birds, fish, and

small mammals as well as bad ones. Enormous amounts of DDT, aldrin, and dieldrin spread over 131,000 acres to kill Japanese beetles in Illinois left the countryside with thousands of dead birds, rabbits, squirrels, muskrats. It killed 90 percent of the area's farm cats as well.

Some pest species seemed to thrive on the stuff. It did them no harm and permitted them to enjoy huge population increases because it killed off their natural enemies. DDT sprayed on 885,000 acres of forest land to destroy caterpillars that damage spruce trees also wiped out ladybugs and other beetles that eat spider mites. Uneaten, the hugely multiplied mite population did far more damage than the caterpillars.

Sometimes, though most of a species died, many individuals survived. Their good luck made them the founders of a tougher breed of the same old pest. The DDT dusting that stopped an Italian typhus epidemic during World War II failed to stop one in Spain in 1948. Malaria-carrying mosquitoes, almost wiped out in Greece in 1946, bounced back a few years later. Scientists working in various parts of the world found only five species of mosquitoes able to stand up against DDT. Four years later there were twenty-eight DDT-resisting species.

Sprayed from ground or air, all pesticides ended up on the earth's surface. Rainfall carried them into river systems and out to sea. Some seeped down to the "underground seas" from which civilized man gets much of his fresh-water supply by drilling wells.

Large amounts remained in the soil, losing their deadly powers very slowly. On lands where they were used year after year, some pesticides kept their strength or increased it.

In less than twenty years the presence of these fantastic chemicals in soil, water, and high-altitude air currents had become worldwide. DDT was being found in fish caught off Iceland and Japan; in arctic sea plants and wildlife; and, a few years later, in the bodies of antarctic fish, gulls, penguins, and seals.

DDT was long lasting in the bodies of animals as well as in the ground. Some of it was eliminated by ordinary body functions. The rest was stored up in the fatty tissue. Grass-eater or flesh-eater, the more a creature ate, the more DDT it stored. Human beings, who ate everything, could not avoid small daily doses of DDT. They got it in the flesh of poultry, cattle, hogs, sheep, and other food animals that had been fed on crops treated with DDT. They also got it directly in many insecticide-sprayed vegetables.

Rachel described a startling incident at Clear Lake, California, to show how pesticides build up in the food chain.

To get rid of gnats, the lake was treated with only .02 parts of DDD (a close relative of DDT) for each million parts of water. The amount found in microscopic plants and animals (plankton) was 5 whole parts per million. In the bodies of grebes, wild birds who ate the fish and died, there was as much as 1,600 parts per million. This treatment of the lake went on for several years.

Meanwhile [Rachel wrote] the nesting colonies of grebes dwindled—from more than 1,000 pairs before the first insecticide treatment began to about 30 pairs in 1960. And even the thirty seem to have nested in vain, for no young grebes had been observed on the lake since the last DDD application . . . . But what of the human being who . . . has . . . caught a string of fish from the waters of Clear Lake and taken them home to fry for supper? What could a heavy dose of DDD, or perhaps repeated doses, do to him?

An important question, but nobody really knew the answer. Human beings could easily be in danger of storing up more DDT than their bodies could safely handle. But what was safe? On the one hand, the pesticide buildup in human tissue didn't seem to be killing anyone outright. On the other hand, what did science really know about the long range effects of these strange chemicals? Without much more experiment, research, and study, there would be no certain answers. And unless the DDT-eaters of the world realized the importance of the whole subject, the answers might be too few and too late.

What science did know was not comforting:

Just a few millionths of parts too much DDT could cause fish and birds to produce eggs that wouldn't hatch, or to hatch offspring that couldn't live. It was happening to eagles as well as chickens.

Some pesticides produced certain types of cancer in laboratory animals.

In other animal experiments, DDT, dieldrin, and chlordane caused liver damage.

Medical journals reported instances of serious—probably permanent—nerve damage to human beings, resulting from careless, ignorant, or accidental exposure to pesticides.

Some chemicals, harmless in their own right, could set up damaging illness in combinations with other chemicals already present in the human body.

The growing resistance of many pest species was forcing the chemists to produce even more powerful poisons in a sort of arms race with nature.

But science also knew that there were biological as well as chemical ways to control pests. Male screw-worm flies sterilized by X rays and turned loose caused female flies to lay sterile eggs. By this method, the pest that burrowed into the hides of cattle was stopped in Florida, Alabama, and Georgia in less than a year and a half.

Biochemistry was producing substances that attracted male moths and destroyed them. Electronics experts and biologists were working together to develop ways of luring pest insects to destruction, or to kill them directly with ultrasonic vibrations. Microbiologists were experimenting with the use of bacteria that produce fatal diseases in particular pest species but are harmless to other life in the environment. And it was sometimes possible, of course, to introduce natural enemies of a pest species to keep it under control.

The last chapter of Rachel's book was a forceful

plea for biological controls that would reduce or do away entirely with the need for poisonous chemicals.

> A truly extraordinary variety of alternatives to the chemical control of insects is available [she wrote]. Some are already in use and have achieved brilliant success. Others are in the stage of laboratory testing. Still others are little more than ideas in the minds of imaginative scientists, waiting for an opportunity to put them to the test. All have this in common: they are *biological* controls, based on understanding of the living organisms they seek to control, and on the whole fabric of life to which these organisms belong.

In the combined work of specialists belonging to many subdivisions of biology—entomologists, pathologists, geneticists, physiologists, biochemists, ecologists—Rachel saw the swift development of a "new science of biotic controls."

This advance, she predicted, could do away with the more primitive kind of science that "has armed itself with the most modern and terrible weapons, and that in turning them against the insects has also turned them against the earth."

Her facts were carefully and honestly marshaled, their meanings made clear; her own opinions were sharply expressed. All she needed was an opening statement to make her readers pay attention. But how? After discussion with Marie Rodell and Paul Brooks, her editor at Houghton Mifflin, she decided to write a first chapter titled "A Fable for Tomorrow."

It was the story of an American town in the midst of a happy, prosperous farming region stricken by a strange misfortune. The town did not actually exist, but inventing it enabled her to tell what could very well happen to real places where there was careless, unscientific, sometimes greedy use of pesticides year after year.

This was a town "where all life seemed to live in harmony with its surroundings." She described the beauty of the grain fields and orchards where, in spring, "white clouds of bloom drifted above the green fields" and in fall, "oak and maple and birch set up a blaze of color that flamed and flickered across a backdrop of pines. Then foxes barked in the hills and deer silently crossed the fields, half hidden in the mists . . . . Even in winter the roadsides were places of beauty where countless birds came to feed . . . ."

It was a countryside, Rachel wrote, famous for the rich numbers and varieties of bird life. People came from afar to see these birds when they crowded the migration flyway in spring and fall. There was good fishing, too, in the pure cool streams running down from the hills. "Then a strange blight crept over the area and everything began to change."

Chickens, cattle, and sheep sickened and died. People began to suffer illness that puzzled the local doctors. "Everywhere was a shadow of death."

There was a strange stillness. The birds, for example—where had they gone? . . . The few birds
seen anywhere were moribund; they trembled vio-
lently and could not fly. It was a spring without
voices. On mornings that had once throbbed with
the dawn chorus of robins, catbirds, doves, jays,
wrens, and scores of other bird voices there was no
sound; only silence lay over the fields and wood and
marsh.

It was happening on the farms, too. Chickens' eggs
didn't hatch. Newborn piglings lived only a few days.
There were no bees to carry pollen from one blos-
soming apple tree to another, and so there would be
no apples.
What had happened?

In the gutters under the eaves and between the
shingles of the roofs, a white granular powder still
showed a few patches; some weeks before it had
fallen like snow upon the roofs and the lawns, the
fields and streams.

No witchcraft, no enemy action had silenced the
rebirth of new life in this stricken world. The people had done it themselves . . . . I know of no
community that has experienced all the misfor-
tunes I describe [Rachel wrote]. Yet, every one of
these disasters has actually happened somewhere,
and many real communities have already suffered a
substantial number of them . . . . What has al-

ready silenced the voices of spring in countless towns in America? This book is an attempt to explain.

At first, she had wanted to call the book *Man Against the Earth*. But reading her newly written opening chapter, she realized that the perfect title would be *Silent Spring*.

Rachel knew she was asking for trouble. Almost 200 million dollars' worth of pesticides were being sold in 1958, the year she began to write the book. Almost half a billion dollars' worth were being sold four years later, when the book appeared. The giant chemical and food-processing industries would consider her book a serious nuisance. Their salaried scientists would go through its pages hunting for molehill errors they could enlarge to mountain size.

"This is an era of specialists," she wrote, "each of whom sees his own problems and is unaware or intolerant of the larger frame into which it fits. It is also an era dominated by industry, in which the right to make a dollar at whatever cost is seldom challenged."

And what of her own large reading public? She knew most of them liked *The Sea Around Us* because it took them "away from the stress and strain of human problems." How would they feel about *this* kind of nature book? She didn't bother guessing. Whether they liked it or not, she had to remind them that there were limits to the biological punishment the earth could take. True, nobody knew what those limits were. But if they were violated, the good old reckless human race might wake up some million days from now to find itself extinct. She had to ask *Mr. and Mrs. Homo Sapiens,* once and for all, if they were sure they knew where their next Earth was coming from.

SILENCE, MISS CARSON!

CAUTION: *Harmful if swallowed. Avoid prolonged breathing of spray mist. Avoid prolonged or repeated contact with skin . . . . Avoid contamination of feed or foodstuffs. Keep out of reach of children . . . . If poisoning should occur,* CALL A PHYSICIAN IMMEDIATELY . . . .
NOTICE: *This material is sold without warranty as to hazards or results.*

—LABEL ON A 4-OUNCE BOTTLE OF 50 PERCENT MALATHION FOR GARDEN USE IN 12 GALLONS OF WATER

"Your unlimited supply of energy rather frightens me," a friend wrote to Rachel in 1951. Ten years later the limits were quite definite. Rachel, unfrightened, recognized them.

"I have been confined to the house since the latter part of January with arthritis," she informed Fon Boardman at Oxford University Press in March 1961. And in June: "I am still at the stage of having to conserve my energy."

That was an understatement. The surgery of the year before had not been entirely successful. But she was fiercely determined to keep the matter to herself. She didn't want the whole world feeling sorry for her.

At best she had only a few more years to live. She meant to spend them freely to make sure the public got something more than "little tranquilizing pills of half truth" about the pesticide situation and about the multiplying variety of threats to the human environment.

She also continued to enjoy the personal pleasures that meant most to her, with tranquility and gentle zest that inspired new admiration in those few close friends who knew of her illness. Summers in Maine . . . teaching Roger how to use her microscope . . . wondering anew with him at the teeming protozoan life in a magnified drop of water . . . visiting the Freemans and their neighbors, Norman and Jacquelyn Berrill, both biologists and writers, both fun to be with. Walking the beach at low tide she could still say with a high school girl's enthusiasm, "Look! A jellyfish!" as though it was the first she had ever seen.

Back in Silver Spring, she listened to symphonic music on her hi-fi system, went for bird-watching walks along the northwest branch of the Patuxent River, and corrected the proofs of *Silent Spring*. Sunday afternoon was a time for visitors, often including her brother Robert and his wife, Vera, who drove in from the small Maryland town in which they had made their home.

Betweentimes she worked on a commencement address, "Of Man and the Stream of Time," which she delivered at Scripps College in Claremont, Cali-

fornia, on June 12. The college had a special meaning
to her because it was associated with the pioneering
Scripps Institution of Oceanography. She looked
forward to the occasion because it gave her still another chance to speak out on the problem to which all
other human problems are tied:

> Man has long talked somewhat arrogantly about
> the conquest of nature; now he has the power to
> achieve his boast. It is our misfortune—it may well
> be our final tragedy—that his power has not been
> tempered with wisdom but has been marked by ir-
> responsibility; that there is all too little awareness
> that man is *part* of nature, and that the price of con-
> quest may well be the destruction of man himself.

She remained hopeful nevertheless, because she
believed that *Homo sapiens,* who had learned *how* to
do so many things, could also learn to stop and in-
quire whether he *should* do some of them.

"Your generation," she concluded, "must come to
terms with the environment. You go out into a world
where mankind is challenged, to prove its maturity
and mastery—not of nature, but of itself. Therein
lies our hope and our destiny."

The next day, while she was still visiting Scripps,
Silent Spring made its first public appearance in the
June 16 issue of *The New Yorker*. It was Part I of a
50,000-word condensation of the book, in three
weekly installments. It would not appear between
hard covers until the end of September, but before

the week was out it was clear that there was nothing silent about *Silent Spring*.

The New Yorker series started a tidal wave of mail to Congress, the Agriculture and Interior departments, the Public Health Service, the Food and Drug Administration, and local and county agencies from coast to coast.

Silent Spring was being discussed in the newspapers—in countless letters from readers and in hundreds of editorials and columns. *The New Yorker* itself had seldom received so much mail about anything it had published. And Rachel's own post-office box in Maine was never big enough to hold the morning delivery.

On Capitol Hill Senator William Proxmire of Wisconsin and Representative John V. Lindsay of New York were reading parts of *Silent Spring* into the *Congressional Record,* and President John F. Kennedy was answering a question. At his news conference on August 29 he was asked by a reporter: "There appears to be a growing concern among scientists as to the possibility of dangerous long-range effects from the widespread use of pesticides. Have you considered asking the Department of Agriculture or the Public Health Service to take a closer look at this?"

"Yes," the President replied, "and I know they already are. I think, particularly, since Miss Carson's book."

The next day it was announced that a special government group had been formed to study various questions about the use and control of pesticides. It was to do its work under the direction of Dr. Jerome B. Weisner, chairman of the President's Science Advisory Committee.

Official book publication day for *Silent Spring* was September 27. Some 150,000 copies were already on their way to Book-of-the-Month Club subscribers. By the end of the year sales would be well over a quarter of a million copies.

The book reviews were overwhelmingly favorable. Hermann J. Muller, Nobel Prize winning biologist, praised the book for calling attention to the "ever-accumulating multitudes of poisons which are permeating the human body on a far wider scale than has generally been realized, with remote effects for the most part still unplumbed."

Loren Eiseley, professor of the history of science at the University of Pennsylvania, wrote: "It is a devastating, heavily documented, relentless attack upon human carelessness, greed, and irresponsibility . . . . It is apparent that man must learn to handle more wisely the products of his own aspiring chemistry . . . ."

Even scientists who tended to question her authority on so broad a subject as this—and there were quite a few—understood what Rachel was driving at; they were sympathetic. A reviewer in *Science,* a weekly magazine published by the American Association for the Advancement of Science, said: "The story of *Silent Spring,* so well told . . . will serve a useful purpose if all concerned with the production, control, and use of pesticides are stimulated to exercise greater care in the protection of public welfare."

United States Supreme Court Justice William O. Douglas called *Silent Spring* "the most important chronicle of this century for the human race."

Perhaps the most far-seeing tribute to *Silent Spring* was paid by ecologist William Vogt. His best-selling *Road to Survival,* written fourteen years earlier, had been a stern reminder that mankind's deadliest natural enemy was man himself.

"*Silent Spring*," Vogt wrote, "could do for chemical pollution of our environment what Upton Sinclair's *The Jungle* did for the Pure Food and Drug Act in 1906." Sinclair's book was a novel that exposed the frighteningly unsanitary conditions in Chicago's meat-packing plants. It shocked the nation—including President Theodore Roosevelt—so deeply, that the federal pure food law was passed less than a year after the book's publication.

The powerful American chemicals, farming, and food-processing industries felt about *Silent Spring* much as the meat packers had felt fifty-five years earlier about *The Jungle.* A *New York Times* article in July made it clear that Miss Carson was poison to the chemicals industry. "SILENT SPRING" IS NOW NOISY SUMMER said the headline. PESTICIDES INDUSTRY UP IN ARMS OVER A NEW BOOK. RACHEL CARSON STIRS CONFLICT—PRODUCERS ARE CRYING "FOUL."

The president of Montrose Chemical Corporation, the nation's largest producer of DDT, complained that Rachel had written not "as a scientist but rather as a fanatic defender of the balance of nature." Furthermore, the *Times* reported:

> Some agricultural and chemical concerns have set their scientists to analyzing Miss Carson's work line by line. Other companies are preparing briefs defending their products. Meetings have been held in Washington and New York. Statements are being drafted and counterattacks planned . . . . The public debate over pesticides is just beginning . . . .

Spokesmen for the chemicals trade associations said: "We are aghast" and "Our members are raising hell." But, one of them added, "We do not intend to answer directly. We don't want to be on the defensive."

What was really upsetting the chemicals industry was identified by Walter Sullivan, *New York Times* science writer, reporting on a meeting of the American Chemical Society: "Despite their distress over *Silent Spring,* the industry men conceded that most of her facts were correct."

Nevertheless, direct attacks on the author as well as on her facts had begun to flow from the typewriters of industry spokesmen before the summer was a month old. They ranged from serious scientific arguments to a long poem whose quality could only have amused its target:

> Rachel, Rachel, we've been hearing
> All the dread words that you've said.

> Were they true and Spring was silent,
> Then I'm sure we'd all be dead.

And, after nine more stanzas:

> Fancy Rachel in her wisdom,
> Brighter than the brightest star,
> Knowing more than all the doctors,
> Time alone her claims can mar.

While they were waiting for time "her claims to mar," two major industry associations doubled their public relations budget and began to flood the nation's press with articles telling the public how beneficial and indispensable pesticides really were. The repeated theme of the articles was that these chemicals were mankind's only sure defense against mass starvation and disease in most of the world. They were also portrayed as the best protection for America's high standard of living. This "positive" approach was accompanied by personal attacks. These did their best to turn the public image of Rachel Carson, distinguished poetic interpreter of the life sciences, into an image of Rachel Carson as nothing more than a sort of middle-aged Nervous Nellie type who had no serious claim on the public's attention. They attached such labels to her as food-faddist, nature nut, bird watcher and antihumanitarian crank. These were intended to discredit her scientific believability; to suggest that her personal tastes and recreations were eccentric; and to hint that at best she had very little in common with "the average American."

"Miss Carson must be one of those peace nuts, too," an angry reader wrote to *The New Yorker*. Another said, "Miss Carson is obviously a Communist. She is opposed to American business. We can live without birds but not without business. As long as we have the H bombs, everything is all right."

Rachel was often accused—and *Time* magazine repeated the accusation—of having written "an emotional and inaccurate outburst." But the long review of *Silent Spring* published in the magazine of the American Chemical Society was hardly a model of academic calmness. It was written by Dr. William J. Darby, professor of biochemistry at Vanderbilt University's medical school, under the headline, SILENCE, MISS CARSON.

"This book should be ignored," Dr. Darby stormed. A few paragraphs later, he urged: "The responsible scientist should read this book to understand the ignorance of those writing on the subject and the educational task which lies ahead." Since they could not very well do both, most scientists were reading rather than ignoring.

Caught on the middle ground of this debate were several important departments and agencies of the federal government. The Department of Agriculture had given great encouragement to the development and use of chemical pesticides because they helped farmers grow bigger, more profitable crops. The Public Health Service was pleased with these cheap materials that supposedly could wipe out sleeping sickness and malaria overnight. The Food and Drug

Administration, whose job it became to keep foods with high pesticide impurities off the market, lacked men and money to do the job well but made no public outcry. Many officials and scientists in these organizations were considerably annoyed by *Silent Spring*. They felt the book, one way or another, was pointing a finger at them.

Only the Department of the Interior offered any serious challenge to the claims of the chemical industry that pesticides were safe if properly used. Interior knew there were questions that needed answering because it was responsible for the well-being of living things in the waters and on the lands of the nation. Its biologists could count the dead fish, the sterile bird eggs, the contaminated clams.

But even Interior, when it complained, was often "shushed" by other agencies. For twenty years, since pesticides had first come into use, the federal government had listened mostly to the voices of the manufacturers, sellers, and large-scale users of pesticides. That's what *The New York Times* had in mind when it said editorially that Miss Carson would deserve a Nobel Prize if her book "helps to arouse public concern to immunize Government agencies against the blandishments of hucksters and enforce adequate controls." By "hucksters" the *Times* meant chemicals-industry spokesmen who were often able to persuade government officials that the new pesticides were not causing any unusual problems.

Deep down Rachel wished she could dawdle sneaker-footed on a southern beach until this fantastic battle wore itself out. She had said her say on pesticides between the covers of her book. Now she found herself having to say it over and over again—dozens of times—in speeches, interviews, specially written newspaper articles, and massive correspondence. Well, so be it. Despite her ill health she could not permit the uproar about her book to drown out the truths it spoke.

Her calendar from the last half of September through the first of November was crowded with reminders that she had miles to go and promises to keep. In New York: a news conference with book reviewers, a meeting with a television producer, her publisher's official "coming out" party for *Silent Spring*, a luncheon meeting of the National Council of Women. In Cleveland: a reception in her honor at the Museum of Natural History, an autographing appearance the next day at Halle Brothers department store. In Washington: an informal talk to the American Association of University Women, a meeting of the National Parks Association, an autographing party at the Audubon Society. In Richmond: a luncheon given by the Association of Virginia Clubs. In between there were more interviews with newspaper and magazine people than she cared to count. The sheer number of them made her realize that she had been forced into fighting a sort of guerrilla warfare with the "anti-Carson" forces. She had been shrugging off personal attacks but answering countless technical questions raised by her critics, one by one. She had been calmly scientific, patient, characteristically ladylike. It was time to change her fighting style. She did, in a carefully prepared speech to the Women's National Press Club on December 5.

She would leave others to judge whether the attacks on *Silent Spring* and its author came "from people who actually have not read the book or from those who find it convenient to misrepresent my position."

The pattern her critics followed was quite clear, however: "One obvious way to try to weaken a cause is to discredit the person who champions it. So the masters of invective and insinuation have been busy: I am a bird lover—a cat lover—a fish lover—a priestess of nature—a devotee of a mystical cult having to do with laws of the universe which my critics consider themselves immune to."

Another piece of the pattern, she said, was to attack statements she had never made. "Anyone who has really read the book knows that I criticize the modern chemical method not because it *controls* harmful insects but because it controls them *badly* and *inefficiently* and creates many dangerous side effects in doing so."

Defenders of the pesticide industry often took another tack, too. They admitted the cases of illness, death, and damage she reported in her book but insisted that these were things of the past. They blandly explained that steps had been taken by industry and government to prevent them in the future. But in her December 5 speech Rachel ticked off seven news stories she had read in the months just before and after her book was published. They showed that the same deadly things were still happening.

A large part of her speech was devoted to discussing the relations between industry and science. Pesticide manufacturers were supporting chemical research in universities, she reminded her hearers. Some giant industrial corporations were financial contributors to various scientific societies. All of this raised questions about the kind of scientific knowledge that was reaching the general public.

"Is industry becoming a screen through which facts must be filtered so that the hard, uncomfortable truths are kept back and only the harmless morsels filter through? I know that many thoughtful scientists are deeply disturbed that their organizations are becoming *fronts* for industry."

In Russia, Rachel said, the science of genetics was being twisted by a researcher named Trofim Lysenko to suit the political ideas of his government. "But here," she concluded, "the tailoring, the screening of basic truth, is done to accommodate to the short-term gain, to serve the gods of profit and production."

Rachel did not feel well enough a week later to deliver the address she had been invited to make at the national Conference on Air Pollution called by the U.S. Public Health Service. She sent it to be read for her.

Her illness was beginning to weigh more heavily upon her. There were times when she simply couldn't walk. At other times, her eyes, which had always looked with wisdom as well as wonder on the world, would not serve her to read a printed page. Yet she continued to make and keep whatever public engagements she could during the early months of the new year. She was unable, in March 1963, to travel to Detroit for the annual meeting of the National Wildlife Federation, which named her "conservationist of the year." Her prepared speech, read by Dr. Clarence Cottam, warned that the problems created by the use of pesticides "must be solved today because much of the damage now being done is irrevocable and tomorrow may be too late."

TO START A FIRE

So this is the little lady who made this big war.

—ABRAHAM LINCOLN TO
HARRIET BEECHER STOWE

Rachel's opponents accused her endlessly of telling "only one side of the story." Actually she wanted both sides told, to the largest possible audience, with complete scientific honesty.

"It is the public that is being asked to assume the risks," she had written. "The public must decide whether it wishes to continue on the present road, and it can do so only when in full possession of the facts."

During the "noisy summer" of 1962, Fred Friendly of CBS News had told Rachel his network wanted to produce a special one-hour television report on the pesticide problem. Would she be willing to appear on the same broadcast with her harshest critics, giving millions of viewers a chance to hear both sides of the story at once? Certainly, she replied. She would like nothing better. Spokesmen for the chemicals industry and for various United States government agencies also agreed to participate, not all of them as will-

ingly as Rachel Carson. Producer-writer Jay Mc-
Mullen worked eight months with a staff of research-
ers, editors, and cameramen to produce the program.

"The Silent Spring of Rachel Carson" was shown
on April 3, 1963. Watching the recorded broadcast
with Roger in her Silver Spring living room, Rachel
was solidly satisfied. It did give the public fuller possession of the facts. Viewers were also stirred by the
dramatic on-screen showdown between Rachel Carson and Dr. Robert White-Stevens, a research executive for the American Cyanamid Company.

The author of *Silent Spring* was a round-faced,
delicate-looking lady with a calm, soft voice and an
easy, sure-of-herself manner. Dr. White-Stevens was
brawny, big-shouldered, bemustached, deep-voiced:

> The major claims of Miss Rachel Carson's book
> are gross distortions of the actual facts, completely
> unsupported by scientific evidence . . . . The
> real threat to the survival of man is in the shape of
> hordes of insects that can denude our forests, sweep
> over our crop lands, ravage our food supply and
> leave in their wake a train of destitution and
> hunger . . . . If man were to faithfully follow the
> teachings of Miss Carson, we would return to the
> Dark Ages, and the insects and vermin would once
> again inherit the earth.

Rachel, unshakable in her knowledge of the subject, replied:

We've heard a great deal about the benefits of pesticides, about their safety, but very little about the hazards, the failures, the inefficiencies . . . . It is not my contention that chemical pesticides must never be used. I do contend that we have allowed these chemicals to be used with little or no advance investigation of their effect on soil, water, wildlife, and man himself.

The United States government spokesmen who had their innings on CBS that evening included Secretary of Agriculture Orville Freeman; Dr. Luther Terry, chief of the Public Health Service; and Commissioner George Larrick of the Food and Drug Administration. Each began by defending the use of pesticides to protect food crops and human health. All of them ended by admitting, one way or another that: (1) Rachel Carson knew what she was talking about. (2) The dangers she warned against were real. (3) The possibility of other dangers, suspected but unproved, needed much more investigation. (4) Stricter control should be exercised to prevent careless and needless use of these chemicals.

Only Dr. White-Stevens, spokesman for the chemicals industry, held out against his frail, cool antagonist, firing one last shot:

Miss Carson maintains that the balance of nature is a major force in the survival of man; whereas the modern scientist believes that man is steadily controlling nature, that he has already disrupted the

balance of nature by his numbers, his cities, his air-
ports and his roads, and the way of his life.

Miss Carson unsmilingly replied:

> Now to these people, apparently, the balance of
> nature is something that was repealed as soon as
> man came on the scene. You might just as well
> assume that you could repeal the law of gravity. The
> balance of nature is built of a series of interrelation-
> ships between living things, and between living
> things and their environment. This doesn't mean
> that we must not attempt to tilt the balance of na-
> ture in our favor; but when we do make this at-
> tempt we must know what we're doing. We must
> know the consequences.

Rachel switched off her television set knowing that
she had won a battle but not the war.

Eight months had gone by since President Kennedy had called for a closer scientific look at the questions raised by *Silent Spring*. At least once during
that time Rachel met with the President's Science
Advisory Committee. Its final statement, however,
was being delayed by disagreements among government agencies with which the committee was obliged
to work.

The committee's 43-page report was made public
on May 15. It mentioned Rachel Carson only once,
but she would not have traded that single mention for
a Nobel Prize. Part of the last paragraph in the com-

mittee's long list of recommendations to the President read:

> . . . Until the publication of *Silent Spring* by Rachel Carson, people were generally unaware of the toxicity [the poisonous nature] of pesticides. The Government should present this information to the public in a way that will make it aware of the dangers while recognizing the value of pesticides.

The entire document was carefully worded to avoid any complaint that it was "anti-chemical": "The use of pesticides must be continued . . . . On the other hand it has now become clear that . . . while they destroy harmful insects and plants, pesticides may also be toxic to beneficial plants and animals, including man."

On page after page, there was strong, direct support for the scientific correctness and public importance of *Silent Spring*. The title of the report was *Use of Pesticides*. It could just as well have been called *Rachel Carson Is Right*.

The CBS television network presented a special follow-up broadcast, "The Verdict on 'The Silent Spring of Rachel Carson.'" Correspondent Eric Sevareid interviewed Rachel in Philadelphia, where she had gone to address a convention of women's clubs. She told him she thought it was "a splendid report." On the air, Sevareid outlined the findings and recommendations of the President's committee and closed the program by saying:

Miss Carson is a scientist and a poet of nature. The men who wrote this report are scientists, period. [Her] book and this report deal with the same facts, the same issues. The first was a cry of alarm from a quietly passionate woman. The second is a sober warning by dispassionate judges. But the cry and the warning bear the same essential message: There is danger in the air, and in the waters and in the soil, and the leaves and the grass. Therefore, both documents tell us, we must know far more about it. We must police it more firmly. There must be many changes in procedures, technical and governmental. There must be new laws and regulations.

Miss Carson had two immediate aims. One was to alert the public; the second, to build a fire under the Government. She accomplished the first aim months ago. Tonight's report by the Presidential panel is *prima facie* evidence that she has also accomplished the second.

Rachel's fire under the government crackled with at least the promise of some purifying results. A subcommittee of the Senate Committee on Government Operations began an investigation that would last for two years. Its job, technically, was to study how government agencies could work together to prevent or reduce various kinds of pollution. It began with the chemical pesticides.

Senator Abraham Ribicoff of Connecticut called the first hearing to order on May 16. The day's chief witness was Dr. Jerome B. Weisner, chairman of the

President's Science Advisory Committee. Testifying a week later, Stewart Udall, Secretary of the Interior, made a point of answering Rachel's critics politely but firmly: "Miss Carson, a far-sighted and alert writer, has awakened the Nation . . . . She has asked a searching series of questions, and her book is a timely warning. Although her critics have protested the inadequacy of certain data cited in her book, they have not, to my knowledge, challenged the fact that she raises genuine issues."

At a third hearing, Secretary of Agriculture Orville M. Freeman defended his department against charges that it was not doing enough to warn pesticide users that they were handling poisonous materials. He explained that his staff was doing its best to educate the public on this point. Actually, it was doing very little. Freeman found it necessary to hide for a moment behind the skirts of the woman whose book had so greatly disturbed his organization: "I believe the public interest stirred by Miss Carson's book, the report of the President's Science Advisory Committee, and these hearings will be of great help in this educational campaign."

Rachel, accompanied by Jeanne Davis, faced the committee to speak for herself two weeks later. Before the session began, Senator Ernest Gruening of Alaska asked her to autograph his copy of *Silent Spring*. The senators paid respectful and admiring attention to her long opening statement. In the question-and-answer period that followed, Rachel's answers were level-headed, expert, and based on up-to-date information. After tiresome months of being on the defensive, she relished the sympathetic attitude and intelligent questions of the committee members. But she was hardly prepared for the tribute Senator Gruening paid her:

> Miss Carson, every once in a while in the history of mankind a book has appeared which has substantially altered the course of history. I think that sometimes those books are in fiction form and sometimes not. One can think of many examples, such as *Uncle Tom's Cabin,* for instance. Your book is of that important character, and I feel you have rendered a tremendous service.

When it was over, Rachel and Mrs. Davis made their way to the Senate restaurant to keep a lunch date with Maurine Neuberger of Oregon. They discussed the two pesticide control bills that Senator Neuberger was sponsoring in the Senate. One would require the Department of Agriculture to consult with the Department of the Interior and state agencies before starting pesticide programs that could be harmful to fish and wildlife. The other bill would require pesticides harmful to fish and wildlife to have labels that said so. Rachel agreed to testify in favor of both bills. She did, two days later, before the Senate Commerce Committee.

Washington and the rolling countryside around Silver Spring were beginning to simmer under the early summer sun. Rachel longed to be off to Maine, but there was still another public engagement to keep. She addressed the convention of the National Council of Women in Washington and accepted the council's first "Woman of Conscience" citation. The honors and awards being heaped on her for *Silent Spring* had a different meaning from those she had received for her three earlier books. The others were recognitions of her personal talents as a writer. These were endorsements of her ideas and her proposals for action on a vital public issue.

EBB TIDE

I heard or seemed to hear the chiding
*   Sea*
Say, Pilgrim, why so late and slow to
*   come?*
Am I not always here, thy summer
*   home?*
Is not my voice thy music, morn and
*   eve?*
My breath thy healthful climate in the
*   heats?*
My touch thy antidote . . . ?

—RALPH WALDO EMERSON

Jeanne Davis drove Rachel, Roger (who was now eleven), and the cat Jeffy to West Southport late in June. On the way, Rachel surrendered herself to the one pleasure that weariness brings—the relief of not having to do anything—not having to read, write, answer the telephone, make public speeches. For a few months she could relax the iron self-discipline that had kept her going through the year since the first *New Yorker* installment of *Silent Spring* had appeared—could it be only a year? Incredible! She felt as though she had lived half a lifetime since then.

Mrs. Davis stayed over for a few days, long enough

to feel the magnetic power that drew Rachel to this place year after year. She could see Rachel's spirits lift . . . Rachel . . . Silverbar the sanderling of *Under the Sea Wind* . . . seeking new strength in the summer riches of northern sea and earth . . .

Rachel's delight in all the familiar living things she saw still held their first-time freshness for her. Contrary to her custom in other summers she did no clambering among the slippery rocks of the big tide pool below her house. But on the long outdoor deck overlooking the water there were always the big events of nature to watch—daybreak, sunset, evening stars, the rising and the setting of the moon, the advancing and retreating tides, the slow-turning color wheel of summer moving toward autumn. Raising her binoculars to watch a distant bird aloft she could still say as though it were her first: "Oh! Look at that tern dive! Straight down!"

Rachel and the Freemans spent a lot of time together. Dorothy, carrying blankets, would walk with her along a smooth path to a nearby clearing carpeted with grass and pine needles. She would spread blankets; then they would lie down and read. Getting to her feet again was hard on Rachel's arthritis-stiffened frame. Once when Dorothy tried to help her, Rachel smiled. "You mustn't think I'm in agony all the time." Then she accepted Dorothy's outstretched hand.

When they weren't reading they talked idly, drawing on their treasury of shared experiences. Edwin Way Teale, the naturalist, and his wife visited

Rachel one summer. How pleased she and the Freemans were that *they* could show the *Teales* parula
warblers nesting in their front yards.

Once, in a tide pool, they found a scarlet sea
cucumber, a warm-water cousin of the starfish, seldom seen in Maine's cool tidal waters. They never
found another.

What had become of the mother skunk who found
good feeding at Rachel's door one night and returned
regularly with her two babies to thrive on Carson
handouts?

Sometimes Rachel would talk steadily for an hour
or more about scientific material she was reading.
Dorothy, listening, was fascinated because Rachel
talked simply, with quiet enthusiasm, transforming
complex science terms into ordinary language.

Once in a while Stanley Freeman would drive his
wife and their friend to Reid State Park for picnics.
But the place that Rachel enjoyed most was the un-
spoiled grounds of a private summer colony at nearby
Newagen. It was a protected area for wild flowers
to grow, for birds to nest, and for native northern
trees to flourish without fear of bulldozers or chain
saws. There the two women wandered as privileged
visitors on winding trails to find themselves facing at
last the great Atlantic sea.

The physical loveliness of the season was made
more so for Rachel by the companionship of the
Freemans and a few other friends. Tactful by nature,
they did not burden Rachel with any needless show of
concern about her health. They successfully avoided

the undertow of anxiety that might have dragged all of them downward through the buoyant surface of the summer's tranquility.

The sun, setting noticeably farther south now, told them what they didn't want to know. It was September, time to think of leaving. Rachel and Dorothy Freeman made one more trip to Newagen. Resting on a bench near the water's edge they steeped their souls in the sunlit beauty of sea and sky, trying to soak up a full winter's supply. Neither of them wanted to speak of the summer's end, both of them knowing that everything ends, sooner or later.

The Freemans left. Rachel and Roger stayed on. When they returned to Silver Spring Roger's school term had already begun; Rachel's desk held a neat stack of correspondence, invitations, and business offers that needed her personal attention.

Walking had become difficult enough to make her use a cane. From time to time she went to her eye doctor for treatment of an eye inflammation, which persisted, but she felt better toward the end of November. She came to New York as her calendar told her she must, to be triply honored in December's first week. Stanley and Dorothy Freeman went with her to keep her company and help her through the strain of the public appearances.

On Tuesday she became the first woman to receive the National Audubon Society's medal, its highest award for achievement in conservation. In her address to the 500 dinner guests assembled at the Hotel Roosevelt, she said, "Conservation is a cause that has no end. There is no point at which we will say 'our work is finished.' "

On Thursday, she was a guest of honor at the dinner meeting of the American Geographical Society at the St. Regis Hotel. She was presented with the society's medal for "distinguished contributions in the fields of conservation and geography."

On Friday morning she attended a meeting of the American Academy of Arts and Letters to hear Lewis Mumford, its president, announce her election as one of the academy's fifty members:

> Rachel Carson is the sixth occupant of chair nineteen . . . last occupied by Lee Lawrie [American sculptor, 1877–1963]. A scientist in the grand literary style of Galileo and Buffon, she has used her scientific insight and moral feeling to quicken our consciousness of living nature and alert us to the calamitous possibility that our short-sighted technological conquests might destroy the very source of our being. Who could better exemplify the humanist tradition of this Academy?

Then there was a quiet, pleasant luncheon for the academy members and invited quests. Afterward Stanley and Dorothy Freeman came to drive her back to the hotel where all three were staying. On the way she reported her experiences with almost girlish delight and apologized for her "shamelessness" in recalling that Mr. Mumford had mentioned her in the same breath with Galileo and Buffon. She was embarrassed because she thought the compliment was extravagant. Exhausted, she rested in her room until it was time to return to Silver Spring. There were Christmas plans to be made, presents to be bought, visitors to be received, pleasant moments to be enjoyed. She looked forward to the holiday.

Rachel and Roger spent the last two days of the old year and the first two days of 1964 with the Freemans in West Bridgewater. On returning home, she wrote to Dorothy, "With your great gifts, as always, you adorned the hours with love and tenderness and with fun and laughter."

In mid-January Dorothy Freeman phoned—stricken, but reluctant to expose her friend to sudden grief. Stanley had died of a heart attack. Rachel, sorrowing for her friends, took little notice of her own affairs for several days.

She moved through the early months of the new year in an uneven cycle of work, inability to work, and sheer painful exhaustion. Weekdays, from nine to four, she could rely on the labors, abilities, and sympathies of Mrs. Ida Sprow, her longtime housekeeper. Evenings and weekends, Rachel continued to prepare meals and cope with the domestic chores from which even professional women seldom escape entirely.

She had no illusions about the state of her health. "It's a war that I will lose in the long run," she said to Dorothy. "But—one battle at a time. I intend to win as many as I can." She would not surrender or retreat. While there was life to be lived she would live it.

At the end of February she prepared for another battle. Surgical treatment had become necessary. She chose to have the work done under the supervision of her friend, Dr. George Crile, at the Cleveland Clinic Hospital. A few weeks later she was home again, under a nurse's care. Early in April Dorothy Freeman received a telephone call from Marie Rodell. Rachel wasn't doing at all well. One of them had better go to Silver Spring to be with her. Dorothy arrived on a Thursday, striving to be her usual staunch, outgoing self, keeping Rachel company and helping to look after Roger.

On Saturday Rachel said to Dorothy, "I've just had a nice thought. I'm going to make a tour around the house." The nurse made Rachel comfortable in a wheelchair and trundled her into the library. Rachel looked around each room she entered as though she had not seen it for years, and in each room she found something that pleased her. In the library: "My, what a lot of books"; in the dining room: "Oh, Ida has laid out my favorite tablecloth."

In the living room she asked the nurse to open a window so that she could talk to her brother, Robert, who was planting rosebushes in the garden. She explained to him that she wanted the plants grouped according to the color combinations they would make when they bloomed.

Comfortably settled in bed once more, Rachel looked up and smiled at her friend. "My, that was nice." Then the two women talked about the coming summer in Maine. "But before that," said Rachel, "you must come back here so we can visit the arboretum in Washington again. Remember that absolute wilderness of azaleas last spring? This time we'll bring a folding wheelchair for me and I'm sure we'll manage quite well."

Two days later, on the evening of April 14, Dorothy received a telephone call from Marie Rodell. Rachel was dead.

Tearfully Dorothy prepared for another journey to Washington. Groping through her desk she found a letter from Rachel, dated September 10, 1963. It recalled the visit they had made a few days earlier to their favorite haunt at Newagen. She stared at the letter without reading it. There was no need. The familiar handwriting, the feel of the paper between her fingers, were enough to rouse painfully clear memory . . .

They had walked through the woods along a narrow path, coming suddenly to a wide horseshoe of beach. Then they sat down on a hard, high-backed bench. The air was cool and moist and ocean-fragrant. The blues of morning, transparent overhead, were deeply dyed and whitecapped on the heaving surface of the sea.

Monarch butterflies had flown past them in their long seasonal migration. Dorothy and Rachel had speculated that few, if any, of these particular butterflies would return the following spring. Rachel, in her letter, mentioned their talk about the monarchs, and the comparison with the course of all life itself, and the naturalness of the end of life.

No individual life, but only Life itself, is infinite. This, because it was the truth, would have to be Dorothy's antidote for grief . . .

She folded the letter, tucked it carefully into her handbag, and set out for Washington. There she joined the world in mourning for the woman whose life and work were a passionate outcry that the earth must not die.

A Selected List of Sources

SUGGESTED READING

BEEBE, WILLIAM. *The Book of Naturalists: An Anthology of the Best in Natural History.* New York: Alfred A. Knopf, Inc., 1943.

BERRILL, N. J. *The Living Tide.* New York: Dodd, Mead & Company, 1951.

BESTON, HENRY. *The Outermost House.* New York: The Viking Press, Inc., 1962.

CARSON, RACHEL. *The Edge of the Sea.* Boston: Houghton Mifflin Company, 1955.

————. *The Sea Around Us,* rev. ed. New York: Oxford University Press, 1961.

————. *The Sense of Wonder.* New York: Harper & Row, Publishers, 1965.

————. *Silent Spring.* Boston: Houghton Mifflin Company, 1962.

————. *Under the Sea Wind,* new ed. New York: Oxford University Press, 1952.

CHAPIN, HENRY, and WALTON-SMITH, F. G. *The Ocean River: The Story of the Gulf Stream.* New York: Charles Scribner's Sons, 1952.

DARWIN, CHARLES. *The Voyage of the Beagle.* New York: Bantam Books, Inc., 1958.

DUGAN, JAMES. *World Beneath the Sea.* Washington, D.C.: National Geographic Society, 1967.

FARB, PETER, and the editors of LIFE. *Ecology.* New York: Time Inc. Book Division, 1963.

FISHER, AILEEN. *Valley of the Smallest: The Life Story of a Shrew.* New York: Thomas Y. Crowell Company, 1966.

HEYERDAHL, THOR. *Kon-Tiki.* New York: Rand McNally & Company, 1950.

MELTZER, MILTON. *The Great Depression 1929–1933.* New York: Alfred A. Knopf, Inc., 1969.

MURPHY, ROBERT CUSHMAN. *Logbook for Grace.* New York: The Macmillan Company, 1947.

SINCLAIR, UPTON. *The Jungle.* New York: Harper & Row, Publishers, 1951.

STEFFANSON, VILHJALMUR. *The Friendly Arctic.* New York: The Macmillan Company, 1943.

STEWART, GEORGE R. *Not So Rich as You Think.* Boston: Houghton Mifflin Company, 1968.

STORER, JOHN H. *The Web of Life.* New York: New American Library, 1956.

WILLIAMSON, HENRY. *Salar the Salmon.* Boston: Little, Brown, and Company, 1936.

INTERVIEWS AND CORRESPONDENCE

In the research on which this biography is based, interviews and correspondence with Rachel Carson's contemporaries are quite as important as more conventional materials. Communication with schoolmates, teachers, townspeople, government service colleagues, literary and scientific workers, and private friends yielded not only factual information but an extra sense of the quality of Rachel Carson's life that impersonal sources alone could not have provided. It should be clear, however, that information drawn from the recall of individuals has not been used without additional confirmation:

For the period 1900–25, in the Allegheny Valley: Minerva Baker, Charles A. Borland, Irene Mills Bradley, Marie Gerino, Isabelle Alter Hendrickson, Charlotte Shallenberger Holland, Gladys Krumpe Lydic, Charlotte Fisher McLain, Matilda Milauskas, George Uhlinger.

For the period 1925–35, at Chatham College and Woods Hole, and at Johns Hopkins and Baltimore universities: Margaret Wooldridge Fifer, Helen Meyers Knox, Mary Kolb, Mary Frye Llewellyn, Betty MacColl, Dorothy Appleby Musser, C. L. Smith, Homer Smith, Dr. Earl K. Wallace.

For various periods in the decades from 1935 to the present, in Washington, New York, Silver Spring, Woods Hole, West Southport, Me., Duxbury, Mass., and other locales: Dr. Frederick S. Bigelow, Fon Boardman, Aubrey Bodine, Roland C. Clement, John Henry Cutler, Jeanne Davis, Philip Dumont, Lee Grove, Jane Howard, Quincy Howe, Lydia Jeffers, Ida K. Johnson, Raymond Johnson, Maria Leiper Miller, William Oman, Dr. Eric Reynolds and (Mrs.) Laura Reynolds, Charlotte Seitlin, Ida Sprow, Clement Vitek, F. G. Walton-Smith, Helen White, and Palmer Williams.

INSTITUTIONAL SOURCES

Note: *All publications of United States government branches, departments, or agencies listed in this bibliography are issued, if in print, through the Government Printing Office and distributed by the Superintendent of Documents, Washington, D.C.*

Washington and Jefferson College, Memorial Library, Washington, Pa. (Mrs. James W. Saxon, reference librarian): Biographical information about Maria McLean Carson and the McLean family.

Allegheny Valley School District, Springdale, Pa. (Mr. John E. McCloskey, supervising principal): Rachel Carson's school records.

New Kensington-Arnold School District, New Kensington, Pa. (Miss Matilda Milauskas): Rachel Carson's school records.

Johns Hopkins University, Baltimore (Irene M. Davis, registrar): Records of Rachel Carson's graduate enrollment and employment. The Milton S. Eisenhower Library: Rachel Carson's M.A. thesis.

Oxford University Press, New York: Data pertaining to the publication histories of *Under the Sea Wind, The Sea Around Us,* and *The Edge of the Sea.*

Yale University, New Haven, Beinecke Rare Book and Manuscript Collection (Donald Gallup, curator, Collection of American Literature): The Rachel Carson Literary Collection.

U.S. Department of the Interior, Washington, D.C. (Ted C. Krell, personnel officer; Rachel C. McCrory, and

Carolyn Frame): Rachel Carson's employment history in the Fish and Wildlife Service. Department of the Interior Library: Texts of publications written by Miss Carson.

The Conservation Foundation, Washington, D.C. (Marvin Zelden, director of information services): Periodicals and newspapers.

Community libraries: New Rochelle, N.Y., main branch; New York Public Library; Rye, N.Y., Free Reading Room; Springdale, Pa., Free Public Library, Inc.; White Plains, N.Y., Public Library.

BOOKS

BAKELESS, JOHN. *The Eyes of Discovery*. New York: Dover Publications, 1961.

BALDWIN, LELAND D. *Pittsburgh: The Story of a City*. University of Pittsburgh Press, 1937.

BANTA, R. E. *The Ohio*. New York: Holt, Rinehart & Winston, 1949.

BARNES, ROBERT D. *Invertebrate Zoology*. Philadelphia: W. B. Saunders, 1963.

BERRILL, N. J. *Inherit the Earth*. New York: Dodd, Mead & Company, 1966.

BUCHSBAUM, RALPH, and MILNE, LORUS J. *The Lower Animals; Living Invertebrates of the World*. New York: Doubleday & Company, Inc., 1963.

COKER, R. E. *This Great and Wide Sea*. New York: Harper & Row, Publishers, 1962.

COMMONER, BARRY. *Science and Survival*. New York: The Viking Press, Inc., 1963.

CONSERVATION FOUNDATION. *Ecology and Chemical*

Pesticides: Notes of Discussions, November 16–17, 1959 (mimeographed and staple-bound). New York; 1960.

COWEN, ROBERT C. *Frontiers of the Sea.* New York: Doubleday & Company, Inc., 1960.

DE ONG, E. L. *Chemical and Natural Control of Pests.* New York: Reinhold Publishing Corporation, 1960.

DYSART, LABERTA. *Chatham College: The First Ninety Years.* Pittsburgh: Chatham College, 1959.

GALTSOFF, DR. PAUL S. *The Story of the Bureau of Commercial Fisheries Biological Laboratory, Woods Hole, Massachusetts.* U.S. Department of the Interior, 1962.

HERBST, JOSEPHINE. *New Green World.* New York: Hastings House, 1954.

History of Allegheny County, Pennsylvania. Chicago: A. Warner & Co., 1889.

KUSART, SARPETTA. *The Allegheny River.* Pittsburgh: Burgum Printing Company, 1938.

MARSH, GEORGE PERKINS. *Man and Nature.* Cambridge: Harvard University Press, 1965 (originally published in 1864).

MATTHIESEN, PETER. *Wildlife in America.* New York: The Viking Press, Inc., 1964.

ODUM, EUGENE P. *Ecology.* New York: Holt, Rinehart & Winston, 1963.

OSBORN, FAIRFIELD. *Our Plundered Planet.* Boston: Little, Brown, and Company, 1968.

PELL, CLAIBORNE, and GOODWIN, H. I. *Challenge of the Seven Seas.* New York: William Morrow and Company, Inc., 1966.

PERRY, JOHN. *Our Polluted World: Can Man Survive?* New York: Franklin Watts, 1967.

President's Science Advisory Committee. *Effective Use of the Sea.* 1966.

———. *Use of Pesticides.* 1963.

RICH, LOUISE DICKINSON. *The Coast of Maine: An Informal History.* New York: Thomas Y. Crowell Company, 1956.

RUDD, ROBERT L. *Pesticides and the Living Landscape.* Madison: University of Wisconsin Press, 1964.

SHEPARD, HAROLD H. *The Chemistry and Action of Insecticides.* New York: McGraw-Hill, Inc., 1951.

SMITH, HOMER W. *From Fish to Philosopher.* New York: Doubleday & Company, Inc., 1961.

STERLING, DOROTHY. *The Outer Lands.* New York: Doubleday & Company, Inc., 1967.

UDALL, STEWART L. *The Quiet Crisis.* New York: Holt, Rinehart & Winston, 1963.

U.S. Department of the Interior. *The Effects of Pesticides on Fish and Wildlife: 1964 Research Findings.* 1965.

———. *Fish, Wildlife, and Pesticides . . . Investigations During 1961 and 1962.* 1963.

———. *Fish Kills by Pollution 1966.* 1967.

———. *Man . . . an ˙Endangered Species?* Conservation Yearbook No. 4. 1968.

———. *Pesticide-Wildlife Studies, 1963.* 1964.

———. *Pesticide-Wildlife Studies by States, Provinces, and Universities; An Annotated List of Investigations Through 1964.* 1965.

———. *Pollution-Caused Fish Kills 1967.* 1968.

———. *The Third Wave: America's New Conservation.* Conservation Yearbook No. 3. 1966.

———. *The United States Fish and Wildlife Service: Its Responsibilities and Functions.* 1960.

U.S. Senate. *Hearings Before the Subcommittee on Re-organization . . . of the Committee on Government Operations: Part I.* 88th Congress, First Session. 1964.

VERRILL, A. E., and SMITH, S. I. *Report upon the Invertebrate Animals of Vineyard Sound and Adjacent Waters.* Washington, D.C.: Government Printing Office, 1874.

VOGT, WILLIAM. *Road to Survival.* New York: William Sloane, 1948.

WALLACE, PAUL A. *Pennsylvania: Seed of a Nation.* New York: Harper & Row, Publishers, 1962.

WAY, FREDERICK, JR. *The Allegheny.* New York: Holt, Rinehart & Winston, 1951.

Works Progress Administration (American Guide Series). *Maine.* Boston: Houghton Mifflin Company, 1937. *Maryland.* New York: Oxford University Press, 1940. *Massachusetts.* Boston: Houghton Mifflin Company, 1937. *Pennsylvania.* New York: Oxford University Press, 1940.

PERIODICALS

Arrow. Chatham College. Various issues 1926–28.

Audubon Magazine. New York. September/October 1963; March/April, July/August 1964; May/June, July/August 1967.

Book Week. New York. March 1, 1964.

Business Week. New York. September 2, 1962.

Chatham Alumnae Recorder. Chatham College. Fall 1956; Fall 1966; Spring 1964.

Chemical and Engineering News. New York. July 23, 1962.

Englicode. Chatham College. Various issues 1926–28.

Frontiers. Philadelphia. October, December 1950; February 1951.

Life. New York. October 12, 1962.

National Agricultural Chemicals Association News and Pesticide Review. Washington, D.C. October 1962.

National Pest Control Association Service Letter. Elizabeth, N.J. August 22, 1962 (Number Spec. G 61–62).

Newsweek. New York. July 16, 1951; June 17, 1963; April 27, 1964.

Nutrition Reviews. New York. January 1963.

Pennsylvanian. Chatham College. Biennial issue, 1928–29.

Perspectives in Biology and Medicine. Chicago. Summer 1963.

Saturday Review. New York. December 3, 1955; September 29, 1962; June 1, 1963; May 16, 1964.

Science. Washington, D.C. May 24, 1963; July 31, 1964; November 18, 1966; May 12, December 22, 1967.

Scientific American. New York. March 1967.

Scientist and Citizen. St. Louis. April, July, October, November 1965; April 1966.

Scripps College Bulletin. Claremont, Calif. July 1962.

Time. New York. September 28, 1962.

NEWSPAPERS

During various periods of her life, Rachel Carson's literary work and her related activities were matters of public attention. This list is obviously not a catalog of specific references within the vast amount of newspaper material of which she was the subject. It is a limited selection of major metropolitan newspapers that reflected her life by reviewing her books, reporting her activities, and publishing editorials about her role as a controversial public figure. The years given for each newspaper are those within which scattered issues or series of issues were consulted.

The Baltimore Sun, 1939, 1951. *Christian Science Monitor, 1963. Newark News,* 1963. New York *Herald Tribune,* 1961–64. *New York Post,* 1962–63. *The New York Times,* 1941–42, 1951–66. *Philadelphia Inquirer,* 1963. *Pittsburgh Post Gazette,* 1962. *Pittsburgh Press,* 1962–63. St. Louis *Post-Dispatch,* 1963. *Wall Street Journal,* 1962–63. *Washington Daily News,* 1962–64. *Washington Post,* 1951, 1962–64. *Washington Star,* 1962–64.

INDEX